ARTS AND CRAFTS JEWELRY IN BOSTON

ARTS AND CRAFTS JEWELRY IN BOSTON

FRANK GARDNER HALE AND HIS CIRCLE

Nonie Gadsden

Meghan Melvin

Emily Stoehrer

MFA PUBLICATIONS
MUSEUM OF FINE ARTS, BOSTON

CONTENTS

DIRECTOR'S FOREWORD

More than one hundred years ago, the Museum of Fine Arts, Boston, played a key role in the development of the Arts and Crafts movement both locally and nationally, by supporting and exhibiting artists and artisans, and sharing the healing power of art with the community. This book offers the first in-depth study dedicated to Boston's influential community of art jewelry makers working in the early twentieth century. Together with the associated exhibition, *Boston Made: Arts and Crafts Jewelry and Metalwork*, we examine jewelry through the story of the artists who made it, the patrons who wore it, and the Arts and Crafts ethos that inspired it.

In 2014, the MFA acquired the design archive of Frank Gardner Hale, a prominent Boston craftsman and national advocate for Arts and Crafts jewelry. This rich resource of images and information has sparked cross-departmental conversations, raised fresh questions, and inspired new research. We are grateful to all of the lenders and sponsors who have made the project possible. Generous support for this publication was provided by the Andrew W. Mellon Publications Fund.

Today, the ideals of the Arts and Crafts movement continue to resonate with the Museum's audiences—connecting people and art to spark creativity, advance the pursuit of knowledge, and encourage cultural understanding. In exploring this jewelry, we encourage readers and visitors to consider their own choices in what they make, what they wear, and what their choices represent.

Matthew Teitelbaum
Ann and Graham Gund Director
Museum of Fine Arts, Boston

THE RISE OF ART JEWELRY IN BOSTON

Nonie Gadsden

In 1901, a writer for the *Boston Globe* introduced the city's readers to the latest fashion in jewelry design: "The vogue of the new 'art' jewelry is now established by the right of the exquisite color and designs of the pieces slowly put forth by the goldsmith. Colored golds, enamels, a fanciful, graceful design, and a few splendid gems are the characteristics that distinguish these new ornaments from the old style set pieces that women have long worn with complete satisfaction.... We can expect to see a complete revolution in the contents of every well supplied jewel box."[1] In fact, this "revolution" in jewelry design was already under way in Boston.

The concept of art jewelry had emerged in Europe in the 1890s in reaction to the elaborate, ostentatious, and frequently machine-manufactured Victorian and Edwardian styles. Often made in matching sets, that jewelry prioritized the intrinsic value of the gemstones, usually diamonds, over the design of their settings; one critic charged that jewelers' work "had gradually lapsed into mere gem-selling."[2] In contrast, art jewelry was conceived as one-of-a-kind works of wearable art that emphasized creative expression through unified design, color harmony, and skilled craftsmanship. Makers of art jewelry, whether independent craftsmen or part of a larger firm, considered themselves artists, not tradesmen.[3]

Art jewelry gained popularity in Boston among wealthy patrons who could afford to purchase their ornaments from London or Paris. By the end of the first decade of the new century, Boston itself had become a hotbed of art jewelry production. In a 1916 article on "Handwrought Jewelry in America" for the nationally circulating *American Magazine of Art*, the Baltimore-based writer Emily E. Graves observed, "Curiously enough, it is in once Puritan Boston that there is now the largest number of artist jewelers."[4] At the time she was writing, the term "artist jeweler" generally referred to independent craftspeople who worked alone or in small workshops to design and create unique personal adornments. Such artist jewelers strove to distinguish their work from the ornaments produced by large commercial jewelry firms, which separated designers from manufacturers and often employed machines to churn out multiple versions of the same design.

Graves's article featured the work of the three Boston artist jewelers she considered to be the strongest. The first name on her list was Frank Gardner Hale, who had become a recognized master in the field of art jewelry for his exquisite designs and expert craftsmanship (fig. 1). Although Hale and his contemporaries had developed a recognizable Boston style of art jewelry and had earned a national reputation, the author thought her readers might be surprised to learn that avant-garde jewelry makers flourished in a city long characterized as prudish and conservative, especially when it came to fashion or the arts. Yet by the turn of the twentieth century, the "once Puritan" city already boasted a vibrant community of artists, craftspeople, scholars, critics, connoisseurs, and patrons, all united by a shared interest in art and design.

The revived attention to artistic quality was part of a larger design reform movement active in Europe and the United States in the second half of the nineteenth century that produced a handful of closely related design philosophies and styles, including the English Arts and Crafts movement and French Art Nouveau. In the United States, different regions of the country created their own interpretations of these theories according to the needs and character of the local community. With strong intellectual and commercial ties to England, Bostonians adhered most closely to the social and ideological tenets of the Arts and Crafts movement.

This movement, combining design and social reform, originated in England as a reaction to the dehumanizing effects of industrialized society on everyday life. Arts and Crafts leaders promoted artistic activity, appreciation of beauty, and making and using handcrafts as essential to leading a joyful and fulfilling life. They exalted the independent craftsperson, praised the dignity of physical labor, and urged followers to seek simplicity and respite in nature, looking to the preindustrial past for lifestyle and design guidance. Arts and Crafts was both an artistic movement and

FIG. 1
A bold, yet delicate necklace by Frank Gardner Hale masterfully combines gold, silver, and a colorful array of gemstones to create a harmonious and unified overall design that epitomizes the Boston look in Arts and Crafts jewelry.

a cultural movement, which encouraged a broader segment of society to embrace this way of life by becoming consumers of artistic wares. One of the movement's leaders, William Morris, famously said, "Have nothing in your houses that you do not know to be useful or believe to be beautiful."[5] In short, proponents believed that making art and incorporating beauty into daily life would bring happiness and contentment to all members of society, rich or poor. As these ideas spread across the Atlantic, Boston quickly became the intellectual hub of the movement in the United States. While in Boston during the 1890s, Frank Gardner Hale was exposed to Arts and Crafts ideals, which eventually inspired him to travel to England and become a jewelry maker (fig. 2).

FIG. 2
In this brooch, Hale deftly combines brilliant blue zircons with diamonds, sapphires, and green peridots in a delicate scrolling gold setting inspired by Renaissance styles.

Arts and Crafts philosophies found a particularly ready audience in intellectual and artisanal circles in Boston. Many core Arts and Crafts tenets echoed the philosophical beliefs of New England Transcendentalism, the first American-grown intellectual movement. As early as the 1830s, leading Transcendentalist thinkers including Ralph Waldo Emerson and Henry David Thoreau had encouraged Americans to counter the cultural anxieties of modern life by promoting self-reliance and the integrity of the individual; the importance of intention and process; and the restorative power and divinity of nature. Transcendentalists urged adherents to cure society's ills through individual and community action. Although Transcendental idealism and optimism waned in American society at large after the atrocities of the nation's Civil War, the philosophy remained strong in Boston's intellectual circles well into the late nineteenth century.[6] It dovetailed naturally with Arts and Crafts concepts, as in Emerson's assertion in his essay entitled "Art" that "Beauty must come back to the useful arts, and the distinction between the fine and useful arts [must be] forgotten."

Thanks in part to Transcendentalist teachings, many nineteenth-century social, political, intellectual, economic, and design reform movements in the United States had their roots in Boston and the surrounding region. Abolition, temperance, and women's rights all originated in New England before the Civil War, and experiments in education reform that began in Massachusetts as early as the 1830s continued well into the twentieth century. Reformers turned their attention to visual culture after the Civil War, hoping to harness the power of the arts to ameliorate the social challenges of modern life.[7] While some believed that widespread knowledge of and appreciation of good art and design would enhance the country's manufacturing success and economic power, others believed in the power of art and beauty to instill morality and inspire joy.

With these aspirations, Boston's cultural elite founded numerous arts-minded organizations and civic programs to heighten the artistic literacy of the city's residents. Under the motto of "Art, Education, Industry," the Museum of Fine Arts, Boston, was incorporated in 1870 as a public repository of art meant to inspire artists, teach historic design, and instill good taste. The Museum, which opened its doors on Copley Square on July 4, 1876, offered free admission on the weekends to encourage visits by all members of the community. The Massachusetts Drawing Act of 1870 required public schools to provide instruction in mechanical drawing, and the Massachusetts Normal Art School, in Boston's Back Bay, was established in 1873 to train art instructors. The Lowell Institute of Practical Design opened in Boston in 1872, and Harvard appointed Charles Eliot Norton the nation's first professor of art history in 1873.

The Massachusetts Institute of Technology (MIT), also originally located in the Back Bay and founded on the principle of providing a hands-on education with practical applications, launched the nation's first School of Architecture in 1868. Eight years later, MIT established the School of Mechanic Arts, a pioneering program in manual arts training to teach basic skills in woodworking, metalworking, and toolmaking that could be applied across trades, academic disciplines, and all aspects of life. Proponents of such programs believed that developing both the hand and the mind would create a more well-rounded individual. After the initial experiments at MIT, other education leaders in Boston began to test manual training courses with children of various ages in public and private schools, as well as in settlement house settings to teach immigrants and the poor.[8]

By the 1890s, Bostonians had melded English Arts and Crafts ideas and native-grown Transcendentalism with the existing progressive educational reform culture in the city into an American version of the Arts and Crafts movement that spread throughout the United States. It aimed to promote well-being by integrating individual artistic expression into the modern world, and instilling the beauty and tranquility of nature in everyday life through art and design. American Arts and Crafts adherents held varying attitudes toward machines: some rejected all mechanical production, while others encouraged mindful and judicious use of the tools of industrial society. The coexistence of these opposing ideas can be confusing to observers expecting to find a unified ideology, but each individual or group chose which Arts and Crafts tenets to follow and how to combine them with concepts from other reform movements. Boston's Arts and Crafts followers, originally composed of the city's scholarly and commercial leaders, at first strove to combine art with industry. As the movement matured, Bostonians increasingly championed handcraftsmanship and the independent artisan.

In New England, the designs that resulted varied depending on the craft involved. The Colonial Revival, a nostalgic interpretation of the styles popular at the time of the country's founding, dominated in crafts that had been practiced in colonial New England and whose models had been preserved by generations, including silver, furniture, architecture, and textiles. Crafts with less local historical precedents, such as book illustration, pottery, glass, and jewelry, had more freedom to experiment with designs from other cultures, past and present. The strongest of these influences in Boston Arts and Crafts came from the arts of China and Japan, medieval and Renaissance Europe, and French Art Nouveau.

Despite Boston's early intellectual leadership in the Arts and Crafts movement, many of these ideas were slow to be put into practice. When Frank Gardner Hale first arrived in Boston in 1896, the concept of "art jewelry" was little known in the United States.[9] European pioneers in the field included the Frenchman René Lalique, who helped revive the art of jewelry making with his flamboyant Art Nouveau designs and technical excellence, and the Englishman Charles Robert Ashbee, who believed that jewelry should reflect wearers' taste and artistic sophistication, not their wealth. While their trailblazing work was gaining attention, the vast majority of high-end jewelry made in the United States still reflected the established preference for diamonds and pearls. Boston's jewelers had built a reputation for expertise in diamond cutting, partly due to the jeweler Henry D. Morse's invention of the brilliant "American cut" of diamond in the 1870s, which maximizes the refractive qualities of the stone.[10] The fifty firms listed as jewelry manufacturers in Polk's *Boston City Directory* for 1897 undoubtedly employed numerous skilled craftsmen, but their talents were directed to the production of commercial, not artistic, wares.

The lack of emphasis on original and innovative designs in all crafts, along with the Boston reformer's interest in improving the lives of the average city resident, inspired local Arts and Crafts proponents to mount the First Exhibition of the Arts and Crafts in April 1897 (fig. 3).[11] The nine members of the organizing committee were drawn from Boston's cultural elite, local architects, and other arts leaders. They had numerous ambitions for the exhibition, including the desire to elevate the status of independent craftspeople and bring their work to the attention of potential consumers, as well as aspirations to improve the designs produced by large commercial firms, by "representing the application of Art to Industry, and comprising manufactured articles and original designs for the same."[12]

The call for submissions listed many craft categories, including furniture, pottery, glass, carpets, silver, book illustration, iron, brass, bronze, and other metalwork, but no specific mention of jewelry. Although jewelry making was implicitly included under the general heading of metalwork, the field was not established enough to warrant its own category. Exhibition organizers did not shun the craft altogether: among the approximately one thousand objects in the show were forty-four examples of jewelry, along with two sketches (fig. 4). All of the jewels were manufactured by Marcus & Co., of New York, and designed by the company's president,

FIG. 3
In the spirit of bringing art into everyday life, Will B. Hunt's poster announcing the first exhibition of Arts and Crafts features custom typography and foliate ornaments.

George E. Marcus. A local newspaper noted that "the designs are entirely original, but a familiarity with the Hindoo, Persian, Egyptian or Pompeiian gold work discloses that ancient models have served as inspiration for these modern pieces."[13] Although Marcus & Co. was a large commercial firm in which design and manufacture were performed by separate craftsmen, the jewelry the company exhibited conformed to Arts and Crafts standards of quality craftsmanship and novel designs based on historical precedent (fig. 5).

The exhibition attracted wide attention. A reporter from the national publication *Time & Hour* revealed the skepticism he had to overcome by observing, "The remarkable thing is that we [the United States] can already make such an excellent showing."[14] The *Boston Advertiser* declared, "There is a strength of imagination, a freedom of design, and a brilliancy of coloring throughout the entire exhibit which plainly bespeaks of the originality of the American mind."[15] The show's success encouraged organizers to establish a permanent organization to support the crafts in Boston. The Society of Arts and Crafts (SAC) was officially incorporated in June 1897, "for the purpose of developing and encouraging higher artistic standards in the handicrafts" through promoting "mutually helpful relations" among

designer, craftsman, and patron.[16] From the start, SAC founders saw the organization as a leader of Arts and Crafts enthusiasts throughout the country, using the Boston crafts community as its testing ground. Many of its early initiatives concentrated on metalwork and jewelry, and during its formative years, the Society of Arts and Crafts helped foster the development of art jewelry more than any other craft in Boston.

But why was jewelry favored? Its uncomfortable relation to the Arts and Crafts emphasis on "useful arts" can make it seem a surprising choice for the Society's attention. Yet the movement's principles were not dogmatically applied, and ideas about them remained fluid and complex. While jewelry may appear not to be useful, it certainly meets William Morris's second criterion of being beautiful. For Arts and Crafts followers, it also could serve as a visible sign of their individuality and their association with the movement's ideals. Successful Arts and Crafts jewelry captured both the artistry of the maker and the personality of the owner.

FIG. 4
Exhibition organizers decorated Copley Hall with greenery swags and potted trees, emphasizing the importance of nature as a design source. The display was crowded with cases packed full and artworks hung cheek by jowl.

Demographic, historical, and logistical factors also contributed to Boston's strength in jewelry making. With the strong participation of the local elite in establishing the Arts and Crafts movement in the city, jewelry makers had a ready, willing, and wealthy clientele. In addition, the city's well--

known history of silversmithing gave Bostonians a deep-rooted respect for fine metalwork. The creations of Boston's storied colonial silversmiths, such as the mint master John Hull and the patriot Paul Revere, were cherished heirlooms preserved in the city's churches and homes. Contemporary silversmiths, such as Arthur J. Stone, quickly became leading examples of how to live out Arts and Crafts ideals (fig. 6). Silver and jewelry, as well as the related specialty of enameling, required many of the same exacting technical skills; their practitioners often shared the same training, and many artisans practiced in both fields. Because of the scale of its products, jewelry making required little space and minimal investment in equipment. The work was not physically arduous or dirty and could be performed in a home environment. And finally, jewelry making allowed for a high degree of personal artistic expression in design and materials, and demand for pieces at various price points was steady. For these reasons, jewelry attracted those aspiring to make a living from a craft as well as numerous amateurs.

FIG. 5
This Islamic-inspired gold and opal necklace, with green garnets and diamonds set in wirework decoration with a fringe of smaller pendants, is similar in style to the jewelry Marcus & Co. displayed at the 1897 Arts and Crafts exhibition.

Jewelry making also offered a distinctive opportunity for women, a demographic newly empowered by the Arts and Crafts movement. In a 1907 newspaper interview, the New York jeweler Edith Vail observed that making jewelry "offers a remunerative field in the larger cities to women with good taste and deft fingers." She continued, "I recommend jewelry making as especially suited to women not only because it is dainty work, requiring skill rather than strength, but because it can be done at home."[17] Some of the earliest artistic jewelry makers were women looking for a creative outlet and the opportunity to be financially self-sufficient. These trailblazers not only promoted design reform, but also advanced the cause of women's rights.

Despite the relatively lower barriers to entrance into jewelry making, finding decent training was still difficult throughout the United States. Members of the Society of Arts and Crafts quickly recognized that in order to achieve their goals they needed to support the proper development of crafts workers. The vast majority of skilled metalworkers who lived in New England at the end of the nineteenth century were employed by large commercial firms – such as Gorham Manufacturing Company in Providence; Reed and Barton in Taunton, Massachusetts; and William Durgin and Co. in Concord, New Hampshire – or by the smaller commercial jewelry companies located on Washington Street in Boston. Yet, in a commercial environment where profits held sway over artistry, few of these craftspeople had the opportunity or ability to design the products they made. Many of them had learned their trade through specialized training in a factory system, or by serving a traditional apprenticeship, either in Europe or the United States. Arts and Crafts leaders felt that modern craftspeople required more comprehensive training: "The success of the ornamental metal worker depends quite as much upon his artistic conceptions and his designs as upon his skill in execution."[18]

FIG. 6
Arthur Stone collaborated with the Boston architect R. Clipston Sturgis to design and make this gold-plated silver communion chalice for Trinity Church. The piece was created in memory of the SAC founding member, artist, and philanthropist Sarah Wyman Whitman; the gemstones mounted in the stem are from her personal collection.

Although the new manual training programs in Boston's schools exposed students to metalworking techniques, they were not designed to cultivate expertise in craft or design skills. Several of the region's post-secondary art schools had begun teaching the history of ornament or design in the 1880s and 1890s, but none of them offered specific courses in metalwork, let alone in the subspecialty of jewelry. Members of the Society advocated for new avenues that offered training both in advanced technical skills and in design for all crafts, using their knowledge, skills, social connections, and influence to encourage the creation of craft-based courses in the city's established art schools. Often these initial training courses concentrated on metalwork, which required less space and lower capital outlays than other crafts such as pottery, woodworking, or glassmaking. The instructors of these new programs were often themselves members of the Society of Arts and Crafts.

In 1901 the Massachusetts native Laurin Hovey Martin was hired to teach a course in "Arts and Crafts" at the Massachusetts Normal Art School (MNAS) on Exeter Street in Boston's Back Bay, as well as a course in metalworking at the Rhode Island School of Design, in Providence. The MNAS annual report described Martin's accommodations: "A small upper room of the school building was equipped for him, where his pupils learn to work their designs in copper and enamel."[19] Martin had studied drawing and painting at the Cowles Art School in Boston before seeking out metals and enamels training in England, first at the Birmingham School of Art and then with the master enameller Alexander Fisher. He brought these rare skills back to Boston in 1899. Soon, Martin's jewelry and enamels were being exhibited throughout the country; a *Baltimore Sun* article of 1908 called Martin "perhaps the greatest handworker on metals in this country" (fig. 7).[20] As one of the first metals instructors in Boston, and indeed in the United States, Martin had a great impact on the development of art jewelry and can be credited with popularizing enameling among Boston artist jewelers, and beyond. Many students from his thirty-eight years of teaching became nationally known

FIG. 7
Laurin Hovey Martin's hand-hammered copper box features a dazzling cloisonné enamel disk depicting a phoenix in tones of green and blue accented with flecks of gold.

for their work in jewelry, metals, and enameling, including Elizabeth Copeland, Frank J. Marshall, Mildred Watkins, and Kenneth Bates.

In 1905 the School of the Museum of Fine Arts started a course in metalsmithing under the direction of the SAC member George J. Hunt (1865/6?–1947). Born in Liverpool, England, Hunt served a seven-year apprenticeship in silversmithing before emigrating to the United States in 1885. He worked in several large commercial firms and returned to Liverpool to run a cooperative Arts and Crafts metalworking shop in 1903–4. Settling back in Boston in 1905, Hunt taught metalworking and jewelry techniques at the Museum School to scores of art students.[21] His characteristic Gothic style and insistence on superior technique can be seen in the work of one of his star pupils, the silversmith Katherine Pratt (fig. 8). In accordance with the ideals of the Arts and Crafts society, both Martin's and Hunt's training was offered within the context of broader art and design instruction.

FIG. 8
George J. Hunt's student, Katherine Pratt, uses Gothic arches and columns to give an architectural presence to her silver box. The blue lapis stones and blue and green enamel on the lid form a design resembling a stained--glass window.

Separate courses were also developed to teach craftspeople who had technical skills but little knowledge of design. In 1899, Denman Waldo Ross, an artist, collector, founding member of the SAC, and lecturer at Harvard, began a summer course on design theory for art educators, design instructors, artists, artisans, and amateurs that offered his theories on "pure design," emphasizing harmony, balance, and rhythm.[22] SAC member Arthur Wesley Dow earned a national reputation in 1899 when he published his methods for teaching art and design in *Composition*. Starting in 1900, Dow taught artists and artisans how to apply his methods at a summer school in his native Ipswich, Massachusetts. Amy M. Sacker, a book designer, illustrator, and painter, taught a course on decorative design at the Cowles Art School in Boston's Back Bay starting in 1894. After the Cowles school closed in 1900, she established her eponymous school of design, which offered instruction in bookbinding, interior decoration, and design in a range of media, including metals, wood, and textiles.[23] The Society of Arts and Crafts offered its own course in design for interested members, Saturday afternoon classes beginning in 1905 taught by Henry Hunt Clark, a former teaching assistant of Denman Ross.[24]

The Society also established a library to provide members with access to instruction manuals and the latest art periodicals. A 1918 inventory of the SAC Library lists several books of interest to aspiring metalworkers and jewelry makers, including H. H. Cunynghame's *Art-Enamelling upon Metal* (1899), H. Wilson's *Silverwork and Jewelry* (1903), Oliver Farrington's *Gems and Gem Minerals* (1903), and George Frederick Kunz's *Gems, Jewelers' Materials, and Ornamental Stones of California* (1905).[25] Numerous arts periodicals of the era, including *The Studio*, *The House Beautiful*, *The Keystone*, and Gustav Stickley's *The Craftsmen*, also introduced readers to the new trends in art jewelry.

In addition to encouraging the development of artistic craftspeople through courses, lectures, and literature, members of the Society of Arts and Crafts specifically supported jewelry makers and fine metalworkers in Boston by establishing experimental collaborative work environments. With the vision and financial assistance of SAC President Arthur Astor Carey, the experimental Handicraft Shop opened in Boston in 1901 as a collaborative workshop where independent makers working in silver, copper, enamels, and leather tooling plied their trades in a cooperative, educational, and noncommercial environment. Designers and master craftspeople learned from one another, fulfilling the Society's objective of "mutually helpful relations," while dividing profits from sales of products of the workshop "according to the relative value of their work."[26] The goal of the project was described in the 1901 SAC Annual Report: "This experiment is particularly interesting as an effort to prove that, even in our day, good work is the natural outcome of right conditions, under which the workman once more becomes a craftsman, and creates objects of art because he puts into his work some evidence of his pleasure in the exercise of his craft." Although the original hope was to expand the number of crafts, by 1906 the shop had narrowed its scope to concentrate on metals and enamels.

At the Handicraft Shop, Mary Catherine Knight, an academically trained designer who had been employed as a silver designer for Gorham, worked alongside the Finnish immigrant silversmith Karl Leinonen and others, as well as an unidentified colleague who was a trained enameller. Knight drew on the varied expertise in the shop to create a unique style of decoration for her silver wares, using leather-tooling equipment to punch out designs in the silver that she then often filled with colorful enamels. Other metalworkers and jewelry makers who worked and trained at the Handicraft Shop in its early years included Frans J. R. Gyllenberg, Seth Ek, George Gebelein, Carl G. Forssen, and Mary Winlock.[27] Although it was founded by SAC members and many of its employees were members as well, the Handicraft Shop had little or no official business relationship with the Society. It was, however, considered a successful example of the Society's influence on the crafts community in Boston and a model worth emulating.[28]

In the SAC Annual Report for 1904, the Committee on Workshops proposed establishing similar collaborative workspaces where craftspeople could rent space and share tools, noting that a "pressing need was to provide facilities for metal-workers."[29] Later that year, a fine-metals workshop opened at 79 Chestnut Street on Beacon Hill, thanks to a $500 loan from the Society's coffers and the generous donation of silversmithing tools by the newly appointed Museum School instructor George J. Hunt. Hunt took one of the seven benches in the shop for his personal work, and the remaining benches were quickly occupied by other SAC members, including the silversmiths Arthur S. Williams and Adolph Kunkler, and the jewelry makers Thorwald C. Christiansen and, starting in 1908, Margaret Rogers.[30] Henry Hunt Clark's class on design for SAC members was held in this workshop, reinforcing the prominence of metalworkers and metalworking in the SAC community. Although the shop was originally financed by the Society, the goal was to make it self-supporting, which was achieved within a year.[31]

Of all of the Society of Arts and Crafts' various initiatives, the Salesroom and Permanent Exhibition, opened in September 1900, had the greatest influence on the development of jewelry making in Boston. To maintain the SAC's goal of promoting "higher artistic standards in the arts," all work displayed and sold in the shop was vetted by a jury, consisting of knowledgeable SAC members including craftsmen, architects, instructors, and patrons, many of whom had taken Charles Eliot Norton's art history classes and Denman Waldo Ross's design course at Harvard. Through its strict standards and prolific criticism, the SAC Jury became a dominant force in shaping the look of the Arts and Crafts movement locally and nationally.[32]

After moving and expanding the sales space several years later, the SAC began holding special exhibitions of individual crafts in the rear gallery of the salesroom to educate visitors as well as encourage purchases. The first exhibition of jewelry and enamels was held in December 1905 and even included older examples of wares to compare to recent work by SAC members. That same year, members of the previously anonymous SAC Jury published their first written commentary and chose to focus on jewelry — but they were not exactly complimentary. After noting the overall "lack of knowledge of proportions . . . of capacity of materials . . . of appreciation for line . . . and of the planning, space, and arrangement of forms, areas and colors" in all media, they singled out jewelry for particularly harsh criticism:

> *Perfectly indiscriminate association and treatment of both metals and stones appears in the jewelry contributed. Silver surrounds odds and ends, scraps of stone which have no intrinsic value, and copper surrounds opals; and as to relative workmanship, too often some of the silver work could be better done in iron. . . . All desire for or knowledge of surface treatment in the metals seems to have expired; they are simply jig-sawed discs into which a stone is planted, and the chains are in most cases puerile to the last degree. In enamelling, the contrast between the transparent and opaque enamels is neglected, and but few rich white or blue opaque pastes ever appear, the enamels resembling some viscous material thoroughly smeared over a surface.*[33]

The jury report for the following year was no better, noting "very little improvement in jewelry during the year. Most of it thoroughly crude and childish in idea."[34] Despite the many opportunities available in Boston for training in design and metalworking, the jury was not satisfied by the majority of the jewelry being produced.

Nonetheless, some of Boston's artistic jewelry makers were already attracting national attention. In November 1906, Claire M. Coburn published "Specimens of Craftsmen Jewelry" in *Good Housekeeping* magazine. She lamented, "The money value of a cluster of diamonds in a ring or a brooch signifies more to the average woman than the design of her ornament, its quality of workmanship, its relation to her hair and complexion and the garments with which she will wear it." In response, she asserted, "People who add to good breeding some artistic feeling, are welcoming handmade jewelry like that shown in the accompanying illustrations, which was made by workers skilled in the technique of the craft, keenly alive to the imaginative possibilities of jewelry and its place among the artistic crafts." All of the jewelry illustrated in her article was made by twelve members of the Society of Arts and Crafts, Boston, and seven of them worked in Boston, including three prominent women makers, Elizabeth Copeland, Josephine Hartwell Shaw, and Margaret Rogers.[35] All three of these early female pioneers came to the field of art jewelry at a mature age, and all had received general arts training before exploring jewelry and metals.

After dropping out of high school, Elizabeth Copeland returned to school at the age of thirty, in 1896, when she enrolled in design courses at the Cowles Art School. She commuted from her parents' farm in rural Bedford, Massachusetts, to Boston three times a week, studying design problems pinned above the ironing board in the kitchen as she performed household chores. Copeland supplemented her art education with metalwork training—probably individual instruction from Laurin Hovey Martin—and developed a specialty in enameling and jewelry making (fig. 9). She claimed she was drawn to these materials by her "intense love of color" and the challenge of working in a previously male-dominated field.[36] In 1901 she started exhibiting her works, and by 1903 she was getting national recognition in *The Craftsman* magazine for developing "a style quite her own."[37]

Josephine Hartwell Shaw, the daughter of a Worcester watchmaker, had a passion for jewelry as a child; in a later interview she said, "I little dreamed... that the time would come when I should be able to create and actually work out in metal my preconceived ideas of what jewelry ought to be."[38] Shaw taught drawing for nearly fifteen years before she started experimenting with making art jewelry, when she moved to Boston after her father's death in 1903. She was able to take advantage of the new opportunities that the Arts and Crafts movement opened up for women and of the growing interest in art jewelry, and quickly found recognition for her work (fig. 10).

Margaret Rogers, a Boston native, studied drawing with Vesper L. George and color theory with Albert Munsell at the Massachusetts Normal Art School in the early 1890s. Nearly a decade later she sought out training in metals (from sources not yet identified) and turned her attention to art jewelry. Rogers drew on her training in drawing, color, and metals to develop her own recognizable style. Her colorful and masterfully executed designs, often abstracted natural motifs, combine precious metals, gems, and enamel to emphasize tonal and surface qualities (fig. 11). Rogers had built a national reputation by the time of the 1906 *Good Housekeeping* article, which published her work alongside that of Copeland and Shaw.

All three of these women also participated in the SAC's tenth anniversary exhibition, held in February 1907. The jewelry section presented 154 ornaments by forty-seven craftspeople and drew some thirteen thousand visitors. That same year, the Metal Worker's Guild became the first craft-based subcommittee of the Society, establishing closer ties among silversmiths, jewelry makers, and other metalworkers. The inaugural president of this new group was a jewelry maker, Gustave Rogers, of Marblehead, Massachusetts — another sign of increased attention to jewelry among Arts and Crafts proponents.[39]

On the evening of December 8, 1907, the Society of Arts and Crafts opened an exhibition of jewelry and small enamels in its rooms at 9 Park Street that displayed work by most of the important American art jewelry makers of the day, including Margaret Rogers, Elizabeth Copeland, Laurin Martin, Gustave Rogers, Florence A. Richmond, Jane Carson (of Cleveland, Ohio), and Mabel W. Luther (of Providence, Rhode Island).[40] The critical reaction was much more positive than the verdict by the SAC Jury two years earlier; one reviewer declared the exhibition to be "the most important showing of jewelry that has been brought together since the arts and crafts movement was launched in this country."[41] Frederick W. Coburn, art critic for *The International Studio*, a national arts magazine, agreed: "Even since the Society's big exhibition in Copley Hall last winter [the tenth anniversary exhibition] a distinct raising of the standard in [jewelry] has been noted — a betterment altogether in the direction of delicacy, refine-

FIG. 9
Elizabeth Copeland's silver box features the cloisonné enameling technique, in which silver wires are soldered to the surface and serve as barriers separating colored enamel pastes. The same wires also form the bezel settings for amethysts incorporated into the design. Copeland left some of the cloisson compartments empty to emphasize the process used to create the piece.

FIG. 10
Josephine Hartwell Shaw exhibited this gold and pearl brooch at the Museum of Fine Arts, Boston, in 1913, and it was purchased for the Museum's collection. Shaw was the first woman jeweler to be represented in the MFA.

ment and, to a considerable extent, distinction."[42] The critic attributed the improvement over the last year to the makers' heeding the previously published "severe remarks" and "censure" by the Society's jury. However, there was another major factor in the change: the arrival of Frank Gardner Hale.

In April 1907, Hale returned to Boston from England, where he had sought out training in art jewelry making and enameling from some of the leaders in the field. Coburn proclaimed, "The *clou* [point of greatest interest] of the whole exhibition, unquestionably, was a large collection of objects from the Copley Square studio of Frank Gardner Hale. These occupied the greater part of one end of the exhibition gallery. They revealed in Mr. Hale a craftsman with an interest in very definite, symmetrical design, which he executes with patience and enthusiasm. The structural side of jewelry making is strongly emphasized in his work." Hale's jewelry featured delicate metalwork that complemented the character and color of his stones and touches of enamel. His work was not overtly bold or flashy, but emphasized expert craftsmanship and more subtle, refined designs based on historic styles (fig. 12). Hale's jewelry was exactly what the Boston Society of Arts and Crafts' leaders had been seeking, as Coburn noted: "Those qualities of good drawing and good workmanship, which the admission jury of the Society of Arts and Crafts has been preaching for many years, seem to be preeminent in his chains and pendants" (fig. 13). Hale's ten years of experience as a graphic designer also are seen in the composition of his pictorial enamel plaques, which he showed either set into silver or copper boxes or framed (fig. 14).

The rise in prestige of Boston art jewelry makers locally and nationally resulted in their rise within the Society of Arts and Crafts as well. In the 1908 Annual Report, the Metal Worker's Guild report stated, "During the past year the Guild has enrolled as members many of the prominent silversmith and jeweller craftsmen residing in or near Boston. The members of this Guild sold about twenty-one percent of the goods sold in the Society's Salesroom during the year.... In view of the importance of its interests the Guild during the year asked the Council for certain changes in policy. Many of these suggestions were acted

FIG. 11
In this pendant, Margaret Rogers combines blue sapphires, purple amethysts, green chrysoprase, and yellow citrines with red glass for a wide range of color and tonal values.

upon by the Council. The Guild believes that the present eminently satisfactory condition of the Society is largely the result of their actions." At meetings and in letters, members of the Metal Worker's Guild stridently advocated for improvements in the salesroom, both in aesthetics and in the knowledge and efficiency of the staff. The guild also revived classes in design and chasing for its members, "blazing a way which the Society may well follow in undertaking educational work among its members."

In 1910, the SAC Jury reluctantly acknowledged some improvement: "The jewelry has fairly emerged from its crude and childlike stage of a few years ago, but much remains to be done before the average becomes satisfactory."[43] By 1914, the jury's lead spokesman, C. Howard Walker, stated "The best of the jewelry is extremely good" — although, he continued, "much lacks contrast, knowledge of form, and texture. A scroll and a small, convex, cordate leaf appear everywhere; stones are not richly grouped; and the Abalone pearl blister and pink quartz cheapen otherwise creditable attempts."[44] The Exhibitions Committee awarded less equivocal praise to an exhibition of jewels and small enamels in March 1913, saying it gave "unmistakable proof of the progress which the jewelry craftsmen have made within the past few

FIG. 12
In another ornament inspired by Renaissance styles, Hale sets gold, citrines, and garnets in gold scrollwork.

FIG. 13
Hale's design drawing for the necklace shows more intricate and complex scrolling metalwork and contains more gemstones than in the final product, illustrating how designs changed in production.

FIG. 14
Hale combines enamel colors and textures with gold foil to emulate the iridescent feathers of the peacock's tail.

FIG. 15
Photographs in the Hale archive reveal that he made several variations of this necklace design. This example is missing the gold or gem-set drops that originally hung from the loops on three corners of the pendant.

years, especially in gold and enamel work."[45] A necklace by Hale with a delicate, pearl-studded chain supporting a diamond-shaped pendant illustrates the type of work they praised: a large, square, ice-blue aquamarine framed in gold and black enamel is surrounded by Renaissance-style overlapping scrollwork highlighted by alternating small aquamarines and pearls (fig. 15). The scrolls at the corners of the pendant are filled with black glossy enamel, defining the overall shape and offering contrast to the lighter gold, blue, and white in the rest of the composition.

A reviewer for the *Boston Transcript* agreed, asserting that the exhibition offered "a fair idea of the present status of the jewelers and enamellers identified with the arts and crafts movement in America" and noting the increase in use of gold and precious stones resulting in designs "conceived in harmony with the rarity and value of the materials, in the direction of a more refined and delicate composition."[46] This description captures the emergence of a "Boston style" of Arts and Crafts jewelry that would become even more dominant in the years to come. Mature Boston Arts and Crafts jewelry is noted for its delicate designs, excellent craftsmanship, and harmonious use of color and materials. Boston work uses gold more than silver and emphasizes bold color combinations with enamels and gemstones, both precious and semiprecious. Delicate scrollwork and vegetal elements compose the settings, and the overall composition of the pieces extends to the chains and the clasps. Boston Arts and Crafts jewelry combined English Arts and Crafts production methods and motifs with some of the materials and flash associated with French Art Nouveau, albeit in a more conservative version. What was said of jewels made by Frank Gardner Hale could also apply to those made by members of his Boston circle: "His work has the sure touch of mastery, and in design and color is beautiful, with a sanity of treatment that makes it perfectly wearable."[47]

THE MAKING OF AN ARTIST JEWELER

Meghan Melvin

Frank Gardner Hale's entry into the Society of Arts and Crafts at the level of Master Craftsman in 1907 was a recognition that set him apart from most other members. They typically remained Craftsmen for the duration of their membership, or gained promotion to Master only after several years.[1] But Hale had returned to Boston with important connections to the Arts and Crafts movement in Great Britain. He had spent a year abroad that included training as a metalsmith and enamel artist at the Guild of Handicraft in the rural Cotswolds, under the leadership of the charismatic architect and social reformer Charles Robert Ashbee. Although Hale spent less than four months with the Guild, his direct exposure to Ashbee's philosophy through this progressive community of craftspeople was to influence him for the rest of his career. Hale credited Ashbee with engendering the craft movement in the United States by having "preached the gospel of the Handicrafts with the guilds of the Middle Ages for their pattern."[2] Ashbee was a highly influential figure within the international Arts and Crafts community, and Hale's hands-on experience at the Guild of Handicraft — followed by an intense period of training and work in London with the jeweler Frederick (Fred) Partridge and his wife, the artist enameller May Partridge — gave him an air of authority that he was to draw on over the course of his career. Hale had first established himself as a graphic designer in Boston, making his rapid transformation into an influential jewelry artist after the trip to England all the more remarkable. The skills and connections needed for such a dramatic career change were provided by Hale's education and professional circles in Boston, as well as his elevated social circle.

Hale's formal art education began close to home in his native Norwich, Connecticut, with study from 1890 to 1894 at the newly founded Norwich Art School (NAS), where he was first exposed to contemporary principles of design and decoration (fig. 16). A school focused on training the modern art professional, the Norwich Art School had close ties to the School of the Museum of Fine Arts (SMFA) in Boston: the noted Bela Lyon Pratt, a Norwich alumnus, taught at the SMFA; and Kate Morse, a graduate of the SMFA, oversaw the decorative design program at Norwich. The practical emphasis of the NAS curriculum and Boston's prominent role in education reform likely motivated the talented young Hale to pursue further studies in Boston, enrolling in the Decorative Design course under Mrs. William Stone in the fall of 1896.[3] Although Hale studied at the SMFA for only a year, he was later considered a notable alumnus.[4] Beyond his formal studies, Hale was also exposed to the Denman Ross System of Design and remained active with the Boston Art Students Association, thereby developing his social network while likely taking advantage of opportunities for classes and exhibitions.[5] Hale was chairman of the costume committee for an elaborate artists' festival in January 1903, where he took the role of a prince in a dance performance. A contemporary review of the event includes an impressive list of participating women arts patrons from Boston's social elite, some of whom were possibly future clients of Hale's.[6]

Following his studies at the SMFA, Hale, like many of his classmates in the Decorations course, became a graphic designer. Among his designs were sheet music covers for the Boston-based music publisher Oliver Ditson Company (fig. 17). He also created designs for wallpaper, book covers, decorative borders, and bookplates for clients including McKinley Music Co., the textbook publisher Ginn & Co., and the *New England Magazine*, a monthly periodical published in Boston.[7] Elements of Hale's graphic design aesthetic, in particular the flattened floral patterning reflecting his lifelong love of flowers and gardens, transposed readily into jewelry designs through sensitive compositions of form and color. Hale's broad exposure to historic ornament

FIG. 16
This portrait photograph of a dapper young Frank Gardner Hale in white tie was taken just a few years after he was a student at the SMFA.

FIG. 17
Many of Hale's colorful sheet music cover designs for the Boston music publisher Oliver Ditson Company are signed, a reflection of his strong identity as an artist. Occasionally he also added the year or, as here, emphasized his role as designer with "Des. by."

is evident in the versatility of his graphic designs, which could incorporate Russian folk art motifs, Renaissance strapwork, or Art Nouveau blossoms.[8] His experience as a graphic designer responding to specific commissions prepared him well for designing and creating custom jewelry.

As an emerging artist, Hale would have followed the development of Arts and Crafts societies in Boston and beyond with interest. Mrs. Stone, his SMFA instructor, was selected to represent the MFA as the committee member who approved entries of wallpapers and carpets in the Society's inaugural exhibition in 1897.[9] Although not yet a member of the Boston SAC, Hale exhibited design drawings at the MFA and at the Society of Arts and Crafts in Minneapolis in 1901.[10] It is likely that he took introductory metalworking classes during this period and also learned to take and develop photographs, a skill that was to serve him well later in promoting his jewelry. The ambitious young Hale seems to have been unfulfilled by the relative monotony of graphic design work. As recounted by his friend and fellow SMFA alumnus

Henry Hunt Clark, Hale decided to give up this line of work and be "no longer dependent upon reproductive processes nor on publishers, but, instead, devote himself to the practice of an art which would allow him to be not only designer but craftsman and producer."[11] Later in life, Hale stated that he went to England because there was no place to study jewelry making in the United States at the time.[12] While this was not entirely true, Clark clarified that as of 1906 "there were no schools in America where the crafts were as well taught as they were in England, nor were there craftsmen, under whom one might study."[13] By training overseas, Hale gained firsthand experience of the established Arts and Crafts communities in England that enabled him to steer the course of the rapidly developing community of jewelers in Boston and beyond. Diaries of Hale's year abroad, as well as later lecture notes and articles, make clear his desire for artistic autonomy and his goal of training as a metalsmith and jeweler.[14]

Hale sailed from Boston to Liverpool, reaching London on May 10, 1906. He quickly made contact with his fellow artisan and SMFA alumnus William (Will) Snelling Hadaway, who had moved to London with his wife, Jean, also a jeweler and metalsmith, at the turn of the century. Thanks to the Hadaways, Hale was quickly exposed to the latest developments in the craft movement, including displays at the London County Council Central School of Arts and Crafts, which had been founded only a decade earlier. Inspired by the couple's work, Hale, with the confident prescience of youth, asserted, "I know this year holds much for me."[15] Hale soon visited the South Kensington Museum, where he had a "glorious time looking at old jewellery and enamels," and went to see historic and literary sites around London.[16]

After two weeks, Hale departed for the Guild of Handicraft community in Chipping Campden, about one hundred miles northwest of London in the Cotswolds area of Gloucestershire (fig. 18). Founded in London in 1888, the cooperative association had moved to the countryside in 1902. Hale described his time in the communal atmosphere of the Guild:

> *It was at the Guild of Handicraft in Chipping Campden that I first started my career as a craftsman, and every day I went to the workshops on Sheep Street, a fine old house, carefully changed with the seasons, and in itself an inspiration to good work and happiness. In Campden, the men were able to have their own cottages and raise enough vegetables for their own use. A number of younger, unmarried men, took up residence at "Braithwaite House," commonly known as the "Guest House," where they were able to entertain their friends*

from town and elsewhere, and all who were generally interested in the work of the guild were welcome, and arrangements were made for their board and lodgings if desired.[17]

Hale arrived at Braithwaite House on May 26, 1906, and was met by Will Hart, a Guild carver.[18] The following day he was taken on a five-mile hike by Will Hart's brother George, a Guild silversmith, an introduction to a life that included free time spent outdoors hiking, cycling, or swimming. His first glimpse of the Guildsmen at work in the shop, "a wonderful place," came a few days later, as he eased into the community's routine by reading and spending time at the Campden Technical School (part of Ashbee's initiative for broader craft education in the local community). Hale visited Ashbee for the first time on May 31 and came away with a surprisingly negative first impression: "Called on Mr. Ashbee I did not like." The following morning Ashbee brought Hale to a Mr. Williams (possibly Edward Williams, secretary) at the Guild workshops, who started him off "hammering up bowls out of copper." Hale found it "an ordeal being sized up by these English workmen," but took an immediate liking to his teacher, Tom Hewson.

FIG. 18
This rare view of the metal shop at the Guild of Handicraft was taken around the time of Hale's stay in Chipping Campden. The photograph is from an album of the craftsman and design instructor H. (Henry) Stuart Michie, who also enjoyed an extended stay at the Guild.

FIG. 19
Charles Robert Ashbee's dramatic peacock brooch, wrought in silver and gold and embellished with blister pearls and diamonds, was widely illustrated in contemporary periodicals. Hale may have seen the brooch in person during his time at the Guild of Handicraft.

Though troubled by homesickness, the sociable Hale integrated quickly into the Guild community. Ashbee and his young wife, Janet, often had Hale and other craftspeople over to their home for meals or to spend the evening "smoking and looking over works printed at Guild," surely of interest to Hale as a graphic designer. Frequent outings to places of note such as Oxford gave him opportunities to see both historic and contemporary art. He was particularly impressed by the monumental Day of Creation series of stained-glass windows by the Pre-Raphaelite Edward Burne-Jones and the Arts and Crafts luminary William Morris at Manchester College.[19]

The Ashbees and the Guild were somewhat of an international artistic attraction. American visitors stopped in regularly, and Hale was pleas-

FIG. 20
These drawings show Hale working out designs of his own jeweled and enameled peacock pendant brooch (pl. 3). Ashbee's design had clearly made a lasting impression.

antly surprised to find that he had friends or acquaintances in common with them. On an excursion with the Ashbees to the Warwick pageant he ran into the extended family of Henry Hunt Clark, who later came to stay at the Guild himself. As a handsome young American, Hale no doubt added novelty to the Ashbees' social circles, as they entertained prominent clients, including the important Hungarian patrons Elsa and Zombor de Szasz. Janet was particularly welcoming of Hale; of one of their frequent musical evenings, he reported, "Mrs. Ashbee played on the spinet & sang old folk songs. She looked very beautiful in a flowing green silk gown."

The lasting influence of Ashbee and the Guild on Hale was primarily philosophical, but some of Ashbee's jewelry designs, such as a striking peacock brooch designed for Janet, made an impression on the younger craftsman. Hale designed and fabricated several versions of a closely related peacock pendant brooch over the course of his career (figs. 19, 20). In contrast to Ashbee's muted palette, Hale's piece incorporates a highly colorful combination of stones and enamel, a signature of the emerging "Boston style" (pl. 3). Hale's peacock pendant brooch was admired throughout his career; a fellow jeweler noted its "almost jazzy arranging of massed color."[20]

After about fifteen days of metalwork training at the Guild, Hale started on his first pieces of silver, a porringer and spoon, the latter a classic Guild design inspired by historic English silver.[21] He would have seen many other examples of Guild silverwork, such as a classic loop-handled porringer with enameled lid and jewel-like finial, a type of object produced in relatively large numbers (fig. 21). Much to Hale's delight, he moved on to an enameling class taught at the Technical School by the skilled William Mark. Much of the enamel work produced at the Guild was brightly colored and simple, but Mark was capable of exceptionally fine workmanship, as seen in a marsh bird hair ornament in plique-à-jour enamel, designed by Ashbee and executed by William Mark and Adolf Gebhardt (fig. 22). Fortunately, or perhaps unfortunately for Hale, the only other student in his class was a Mr. Davenport, "a conceited ass" (so Hale reported in his diary) from the printed books department at the British Museum, who had arrived for a two-week stay with his family. Hale's dislike of his lone classmate was offset by his excitement with enameling, which he called "the most interesting work I ever attempted." Within some seven days, Hale had completed an enamel stork, followed by his first piece of champlevé enamel.

As his time at the Guild drew to a close, Hale got into an argument with Mr. Williams in the metalwork shop over ownership of the pieces he had made. Self-assured and with a proprietary instinct for his artwork, Hale noted that Williams "insisted they should belong to the Guild but I insisted on owning them on payment of cost of materials & won out." The Guild maintained a gallery and showroom in London and relied in part on sales of its products for monetary support. Hale's stay coincided with a shift in the Guild's business model, intended to shore up the growing financial losses, so he should have been aware of the effect of retaining his pieces. Hale also consulted James Webster, the newly appointed Guild manager brought in to stabilize its finances, about returning to the Guild silver workshop the following week. Webster approved his request and also took two enamels for retail, suggesting that Hale's work was reasonably accomplished. After settling his accounts, noting the price of silver, and completing his notes on silversmithing and enameling, Hale threw himself into enameling — "Worked all day & nearly melted working with the intense heat of the furnace" — and completed what was likely a plaque, featuring "fishes, the first really successful piece I've made." Tasked with a range of projects,

FIG. 21
This porringer is a classic example of Ashbee's simple but dramatic design aesthetic, with its hammered surface, elongated loop handles, and enameled lid with a jewel-like blister pearl finial. It exemplifies the metalwork and enameling Hale was trained to emulate at the Guild.

FIG. 22
A finely enameled hair ornament (later converted to a brooch), with its backless enamel cells—essentially a miniature stained-glass window—is one of the most sophisticated ornaments made at the Guild of Handicraft.

some as minor as enameling a thimble, he quickly gained proficiency, and soon it took him less than a week to make an enamel work depicting a thistle. Back in the silver shop, Hale worked so hard that he blistered his hands engraving a ship on a silver buckle. He started learning silver chasing under Arthur Penny, also using the opportunity of being back in the metal workshop to make settings for his enamels, with many evenings devoted to making design drawings.

Enameling remained a lifelong passion of Hale's, and he considered himself a jeweler and an enameller in equal measure (figs. 23, 24). He returned to early subjects, such as compositions with fish, frequently throughout his career (pl. 10). In some respects, his brilliant Limoges enamels reveal his strength as a colorist even more than his jewelry does. Galleons in full sail, a popular contemporary subject, are infused with a painterly dynamism, and Hale's love for all things medieval is reflected in his choosing to exhibit a plaque depicting a knight on horseback as late as 1941 (pls. 8–11).[22]

Hale's time at the Guild ended with the much anticipated arrival of his friend and former housemate, the composer and Ditson music editor Charles Fonteyn (Carl) Manney, and a rousing send-off from the Guilds-

FIGS. 23 AND 24
The enamel plaques set in hammered metal boxes of copper and silver are of the type that Hale described making toward the end of his stay at the Guild.

men. Setting off on vacation with Manney, Hale hoped to secure an internship with a jeweler in Switzerland or France, after enjoying the sights in the Netherlands and Germany. Ever observant and with an eye for detail, Hale admired the women's lace headgear and gold ornaments in Rotterdam; in Bonn he and Carl stayed at the Hamburger Hof hotel, decorated in the "Art Nouveau of the maddest kind." In Geneva, Hale began making serious inquiries, visiting a Monsieur Durand to ask about "studying at his school (evenings)." He called in on local jewelers to see if they could take him as a student for three months, but without success. When the two moved on to Paris, they found much to satisfy their shared interest in art and architecture; highlights included the Puvis de Chavannes decorations at the Pantheon and Rodin's *Thinker*. Seemingly on a tighter budget than Carl, who attended concerts every evening, Hale focused on his professional prospects. He spent long hours visiting jewelers, including Tiffany's and Gorham, up through his last day in Paris.

Upon arriving in London, Hale immediately went to visit a selling exhibition of Arts and Crafts at the Grafton Galleries, where he inquired about studying with the metalworkers Nancy Agar and John Bonnor.[23] He found his most important teacher shortly thereafter, when Will Hadaway introduced him to the noted jeweler and former Guild member Fred Partridge. The two quickly came to an agreement for Hale to pay Partridge one pound a week for instruction, considerably less than the one hundred pounds for six months' teaching that Bonnor asked. Having secured accommodation near Partridge's studio, Hale spent his first day preparing his workbench, making a blowpipe, and buying supplies. Plucknett's (a jewelry and watchmaking establishment) provided general supplies and silver chain, Montague Fordham's gallery or workshop furnished gemstones, and Hale obtained silver and gold solder from a dental manufacturer. Within a week, Hale started work on his first brooch and made a turquoise pendant two weeks later. Hale spent long days at Partridge's studio, frequently attended concerts and plays, and in the evening, when not at work, read about jewelry and design or drew sheet music covers for Ditson. He made frequent outings to the South Kensington Museum to study and sketch the jewelry collection, occasionally buying images from their shop for reference.

On his birthday in November, Fred and May Partridge gave Hale two sapphires. He also received a promised gift of $400 (approximately $10,000 today) from a source he referred to as "J," to help him finish out his year of study. Compared to the enviable work-life balance he enjoyed at the Guild of Handicraft, Hale's pace of life in London was intense. Taking advantage of every opportunity afforded him, Hale also started attending evening lessons in repoussé and chasing at the Sir John Cass Technical Institute, known as the Cass. Much as the Ashbees had, May and Fred Partridge took Hale under their wing, although the relationship was not without friction; Hale confronted his mentors in early December for not being sufficiently present. After two months of intense work, Hale traveled to Scotland to spend Christmas with Alec Miller, his good friend from the

Guild of Handicraft. Reflecting his keen interest in the contemporary art scene, Hale's short visit to Scotland included visits to art galleries to see Whistler portraits and tea at Miss Cranston's avant-garde Art Tea Shop. In the New Year, Hale immediately resumed paid work on sheet music covers, a necessary distraction even with generous financial support from "J." He started working on a brooch for his friend and future wife, Julia Dwight, while also devoting more time to designing jewelry.

In preparing for his return to the United States, Hale began strategically calculating which tools and materials he could bring back without incurring import duties, even visiting the American consul for advice. A week before setting sail, Hale went shopping for enamels, a furnace, and tools worth about two pounds. The time spent working with Partridge had a strong influence on Hale's development as a jeweler. Like many artisan jewelers of the day, Partridge favored compositions with moonstones, and his carefully wrought ornaments often included delicate enamel decoration, possibly by his wife, May, a skilled enamel artist (fig. 25). Some of Hale's early designs also feature these glowing white stones, which offset to some extent the relatively rudimentary metalwork in pewter or silver, typically finished with a simple rope twist (fig. 26).

Although Julia didn't marry Hale until 1909, her financial support may have enabled Hale to embark on a career as a jewelry designer and maker upon his return to Boston in 1907 – a decision that left his family, by one account, "grieved, amazed and shocked."[24] He first set up shop at 400 Northampton Street, in the same building as the master enamel artist Laurin Hovey Martin. By the end of the year Hale was exhibiting large numbers of jewelry pieces in Boston and at the Rhode Island School of Design.[25] The following spring, Hale's work was included in a special exhibition at the Society of Arts and Crafts in Boston on English craftwork. Among the more than one hundred pieces on display, Hale's jewels received special mention, along with those by the Tuscan jeweler Edgar Perera. *American Art News* described both as well-known craftsmen, reflecting Hale's rapid rise in less than a year.[26] Hale's body of work was substantial, reaching hundreds of objects in the course of thirty years, as evidenced by his archive. His early works display elements of his mature style, typically incorporating foliate elements and featuring colorful stones, cameos, or enamel panels. His commitment to documentation of his productions through drawings and photographs, and his strong desire to establish and promote an individual artistic identity, led to the preservation of his early designs (fig. 27).

FIG. 25
This luminous moonstone and enamel necklace with four stylized butterflies represents the work of the master jeweler Frederick Partridge—with possible contributions by his wife, May Partridge—at its finest. Hale's intimate exposure to the couple's studio and their sophisticated craft helped accelerate his rapid development as a jeweler.

FIG. 26
An early pewter and moonstone pendant with a rope twist finish reflects Hale's metalwork training in the English tradition.

By 1913, the year he moved his workshop to what would become his long-term business address at 2 Park Square, Hale had joined a number of SAC committees: the Auxiliary Committee on Craftsmen Membership, the Library committee (which curiously suggested that the SAC consider a New York retail outlet), and perhaps most important, the exhibition jury. That same year, the Jury Committee reported on a limited number of "super--excellent examples of jewelry," which likely included Hale's work; his jewelry continued to be singled out by the jury for years to come. He remained active on the committees until 1918, when the Jewelers' Guild emerged with him as its leader. Essentially a professional advocacy group under the

FIG. 27
Several of the jewels pictured here appeared in reviews of Hale's early exhibitions. Although the photographs, likely taken and developed by Hale, were reproduced only in black and white, Hale took great care to tint the prints by hand to indicate his choice of stones.

umbrella of the larger Society, the Guild provided an opportunity for members to reconnect with the founding ideals of the Society, which Hale felt had become obscured by day-to-day commercial operations. He expressed the hope in the SAC annual report published in 1928 that all jeweler members would join the Jewelers' Guild, because "there was a certain power in numbers," and because it was "an ideal organization for promoting good fellowship, and a means of setting high standards for design and workmanship."

Hale quickly established a pattern of participating in selling exhibitions, typically for one or two weeks in the spring (April or May) and early winter (November or December), the latter to capitalize on holiday commerce. A frequent exhibitor with the SAC, Hale also showed his work at independent galleries, sometimes simultaneously in different cities, to gain coverage in the press and contemporary periodicals. For example, in May 1914 he participated in the SAC ecclesiastical exhibition, where his crosses were singled out for praise (along with examples by Josephine Hartwell Shaw), as well as in a joint exhibition with Margaret Rogers at the Little Gallery in New York. Most of the time he exhibited jewelry, almost always described as handwrought, along with enamels, but he also organized separate displays of each. Hale sometimes exhibited at different galleries in a city within the same year, as in New York in 1915, when his jewelry was featured at the Little Gallery and the Ehrich Galleries.

The years 1915 to 1917 saw a turning point in Hale's career, when several important awards, including the SAC bronze medal in 1915, helped to establish his position on the national stage. During this period he began to appear more frequently across the country, embarking on a multiweek circuit of lectures and brief selling exhibitions of his work. His increased visibility helped him develop a national clientele, including a particularly devoted group of clients in Pittsburgh. Hale remained committed to supporting and promoting the teaching of craft in schools, as he made time to speak with local craftspeople and students while touring. As much as he was focused on his individual artistic path, he was dedicated to promoting the value of craftsmanship in society. Throughout his career, Hale engaged fellow artisans in his studio; within its first five years, John Ballou and Edward Everett Oakes had begun working with Hale (fig. 28).

Around 1918 Hale took on as an assistant a military veteran and former coal miner from West Virginia. The man had received some jewelry training as part of his rehabilitation and wished to pursue jewelry making as a profession. Hale's embrace of a disabled craftsman underscores his belief in the holistic benefits of the Arts and Crafts movement. Also in the tradition of

the movement, Hale worked closely with many women artists throughout his career, including Gertrude Rosendahl of Brockton, Massachusetts, and Helen Maxton Holms, from Norwich, Connecticut, as well as short-term students such as Marjorie Whitney in the summer of 1935.[27] In doing so, he re-created the learning environment he had benefited from in his early days. A prolific jeweler, a prominent figure within the Society of Arts and Crafts and Jewelers' Guild, and a celebrated national speaker, Hale continued to be a significant influence for more than three decades, shaping the work of his fellow artists in theory and in practice.

FIG. 28
This photograph shows Edward Everett Oakes, John Ballou, and Hale (left to right), most likely in Hale's Southampton Street workshop, about 1909.

GALLERY

PLATE I

The balanced form and fine execution of this elegant tourmaline pendant framed in gold reflect Hale's strong foundation in design.

PLATE 2
The scrolling gold setting for a striking yellow sapphire and diamond brooch is strongly reminiscent of Hale's decorative frames on sheet music covers.

PLATE 3
Hale's peacock pendant brooch was one of his most celebrated designs. His design drawings help clarify alterations made over time to this fragile piece, most likely by Hale himself.

PLATE 4

The metalwork in Hale's ornaments frequently incorporates stylized leaves, as in this foliate gold brooch set with sapphires and diamonds. The maker's attention to detail is evident in the playful transition in scale, with the round diamonds diminishing to gold beads.

PLATE 5

Hale's strength as a colorist is evident in even this diminutive pendant, where the careful choice of tourmaline and peridot highlights the opalescent palette of the central pearl.

PLATE 6
An opal pendant, framed by scrolling gold elements accented with sapphires and green garnets and Hale's signature grape clusters, is one of the foremost examples of the colorful "Boston look."

PLATE 7
The subtle differences between Hale's carefully composed drawing and the finished piece show how the design evolved as the pendant was executed.

Hale

PLATES 8–11

Hale turned frequently to the art and culture of the Middle Ages and Renaissance for inspiration in his jewel-toned enamels. The rich palette of his knight on horseback with a townscape in the distance recalls manuscript illuminations, and the visual impact of a galleon in full sail or the oars of a Viking longship plying the ocean provides dramatic effect within tightly cropped compositions.

F.G.Hale

F.C.Hale

THE BOSTON LOOK AND ITS CREATORS

Emily Stoehrer

In 1909, two years after Frank Gardner Hale returned to Boston from England, he hired a young assistant named Edward Everett Oakes. The novice spent the next five years learning from Hale and making handwrought jewelry under the Hale name. When Oakes left Hale's studio in 1914, he joined the bench at Josephine Hartwell Shaw's new Duxbury workshop, Three Acres, located about thirty-five miles outside Boston. Although Oakes may have been in the background for consumers of these glittering ornaments, his work was known to members of the Society of Arts and Crafts, which elevated him to Master Craftsmen status in 1917. The following year Oakes opened his own workshop and hired his own assistant, Elsie Parsons, thus initiating the second generation of Boston Arts and Crafts jewelers.

The relationship of Oakes with his mentors Hale and Shaw is just one example of the collaborative environment for craftspeople in Boston in the early twentieth century.[1] The spirit of cooperation is evident in the tangled lineage of the region's jewelers and was documented in the "Principles of Handicraft" that prefaced Society of Arts and Crafts annual reports — calling for "artistic cooperation" and stating, "When the designer and the workman are not united in the same person, they should work together, each teaching the other his own special knowledge, so the faculties of the designer and the workman may tend to become united in each other."[2] During the first three decades of the twentieth century, Boston also became a center for Arts and Crafts education.

These educational and collaborative initiatives produced a recognizable style of jewelry making, noted for uniting design and handcraftsmanship as well as for its use of color and precious materials. The "Boston look" tended to be glitzier than that of jewelry designed in other Arts and Crafts centers, such as Chicago. Jewels from Boston combine gemstones or enamel with scrolling metalwork in platinum, gold, and silver, and have such a consistent look that it can be difficult to recognize which of the city's designer-craftspeople created them. Many of these artists received the same education and had teachers in common: local schools and technical programs, along with a vibrant apprenticeship system, aided in training a generation of jewelers that in addition to Hale, Shaw, and Oakes included Lucretia McMurtrie Bush, Elizabeth Copeland, Jessie Ames Dunbar, Hazel Blake French, Margaret Rogers, and Gertrude Twichell. Society of Arts and Crafts records, newspaper advertisements, and magazine articles attest that these Boston artists were prolific in their production and were celebrated in their lifetimes. However, relatively few known examples of work by these jewelers exists today. By tracing the interlocking careers of these teachers and students, and by closely examining design drawings along with the surviving jewelry, it becomes possible to identify similarities and differences in their work.

Some of the first-generation Boston jewelers are united by the instruction of Denman Ross. He counted Elizabeth Copeland, Frank Gardner Hale, and Josephine Hartwell Shaw among his students. Ross believed that art education should train the eye, guiding students in the principles and elements of design with the goal of increasing "the perception and appreciation of Order, the sense of Beauty."[3] He taught artists to think, not to make; the making would be the natural result of an education in design.

What may have seemed natural to Ross required years of manual and technical instruction and practice. Complementing Ross's lectures was hands-on work in classroom studios like that of Laurin Hovey Martin at the Massachusetts Normal Art School and George J. Hunt at the School of the Museum of Fine Arts, as well as private instruction offered by Amy Sacker and others.[4] After formal training, or in lieu of it, some craftsmen — like Oakes — opted for an apprenticeship to a master jeweler. These educational options helped guide aspiring craftspeople toward a career in jewelry (fig. 29).

As a founding member of the Society of Arts and Crafts, and an early donor to the MFA, Ross helped shape the Museum's collection and the city's creative landscape. Ross's writings and lectures emphasized harmony,

FIG. 29
George Hunt instructs metals students at the School of the Museum of Fine Arts. The segregated classroom has women on one side and men on the other.

balance, and rhythm, as well as color and composition in design. In a small circle, in a relatively small city, Ross's influence would have been pervasive. He believed strongly that viewing works of art in museum study rooms and galleries was an essential part of design education. Free entrance to the MFA was one of the benefits of a Society of Arts and Crafts membership. The influence of both Ross's ideas and the Museum's collection would have been significant for Boston jewelers, regardless of their training.

Josephine Shaw had trained and worked in Boston, New York, and Philadelphia as an art educator before taking Ross's summer course at Harvard. Under the guidance of Arthur Wesley Dow at the Pratt Institute in Brooklyn, Shaw developed an appreciation for Asian art, likely deepened by Denman Ross's course, and launched a career in metalsmithing in 1905. From 1915 to 1920 – when Oakes was working for her – Shaw made some of her largest and most significant work.[5] Her interest in an Eastern aesthetic is evident in a substantial necklace with two large central jade elements likely taken from a Chinese artifact (pl. 13). In a 1915 article in *House Beautiful*, Shaw described how, in making jewels, the stone "suggests the setting"; Oakes echoed this idea years later when he reflected that "in jewelry it may be that the stone or stones suggest the design and then again it may be the design calls for certain gems."[6]

The use of colorful and unusual gemstones sets Boston jewelry apart. In addition to receiving an education in design and metalwork, Boston jewelers shared a keen awareness of gems and interest in their historical use. The Society of Art and Crafts helped educate and inspire its members through lectures, such as one presented in 1910 on "Precious Stones, Their Manipulation and Their Application in the Arts" by the country's foremost expert, Dr. George Frederick Kunz, chief gemologist at Tiffany & Co.[7] Frank Gardner Hale prepared a lecture titled "The Value and Romance of Precious and Semi-Precious Stones," presenting the mythology surrounding diamonds, emeralds, rubies, sapphires, and pearls.[8] Oakes had a lifelong fascination with gems and minerals sparked by an uncle who was a lapidary.[9] Many Boston jewelers sourced gemstones from dealers or stone cutters in New York. They strove to use these gems, along with the enamels they also favored, in a way that was integral to the pieces' artistic harmony.

The style of jewelry that developed in Boston was guided by the jurying process conducted by the Society of Arts and Crafts.[10] As a recognizable look evolved, subtle differences emerged between makers. In the six known surviving examples of Josephine Shaw's jewelry, colorful gemstones or gemlike materials are the focal point. In keeping with her description of her design methods, the gemstones appear to have been the starting point for the design, with the metalwork intended to highlight the natural beauty of a single stone or, often, a cluster of stones in a single color way. In two necklaces, one with a cross pendant that the artist donated to the Museum of Fine Arts in 1914 (pl. 17), and another with carved gemstones probably designed a few years later (pl. 13), Shaw chose a group of pink and purple gems. In all of her surviving work, the gems are bezel set, with metal circling the entire gemstone. While some British Arts and Crafts jewelers used prong settings, bezel setting, which allows for greater saturation of color, was favored by Boston jewelers.

At the Society's tenth-anniversary exhibition in 1907, among the more than forty jewelers showing alongside Josephine Shaw were Margaret Rogers and Elizabeth Copeland. In this exhibition, each piece was given a letter classification. Work labeled "A" was designed and made by a single craftsman, "B" indicated a collaborative effort designed and made by two craftsman, "C" meant that more than two designers or craftsmen participated in the design and execution of an object, and "D" meant that works were designed by the exhibitor and fabricated in an anonymous "factory system."[11] Notably, each work by Copeland, Shaw, and Rogers met the "A" standard.

The work of Margaret Rogers is similar at first glance to that of Hale and Shaw, but there are subtle differences. Her chosen colors have a greater variety, and her design formula is more consistent. Brooches have a large central stone circled by smaller colored stones, and necklaces alternate cabochon-cut gemstones with smaller stones surrounded by decorative metalwork often with a floral motif (pl. 18). Rogers studied and loved color and gemstones and it's as if an article in *Vogue* was speaking of her work when it proclaimed in 1921 that "metal must be absent to the eye. It is jewels and not metals that have the urgent call at present."[12] Sometimes her austere metalwork appears to be simply a way to hold the stones in place (pl. 19). While Rogers's work is more restrained, her work as a colorist is similar to that of her British counterparts Dorrie Nossiter and Sibyl Dunlop, who also created vibrant ornaments with dynamic color selections.

Elizabeth Copeland displayed six ornaments in the decennial exhibition. Educated at the Cowles Art School in Boston, Copeland took design classes from Amy Sacker, may have had private lessons from Laurin Hovey Martin, and studied with Denman Ross at Harvard. Like Hale, she also traveled to London, refining her skills under the tutelage of the master enameller Alexander Fisher. Clients who were familiar with her enameled metalwork may have been surprised that her jewelry from 1907 did not feature enamel. One surviving brooch — made around that time, but not included in the exhibit — is designed around an oval turquoise gemstone with a gold frame and leaves terminating in a radiant opal drop (pl. 20). The shape and color of the piece are similar to those of a brooch worn in a portrait of the artist William McGregor Paxton's mother, Rose (fig. 30). She may have been one of the many patrons who appreciated this style of jewelry; it's also possible that Paxton — who was an instructor at the School of the Museum of Fine Arts — added the brooch to help promote the work of these jewelers.

The followers of Shaw, Rogers, Copeland, and Hale make up the second generation of Boston jewelers. As the city's craft education system

expanded to produce new jewelers, the first-generation makers presented their work alongside a new group that included Lucretia McMurtie Bush, Gertrude Twichell, and Edward Everett Oakes. These makers built on the style established by their predecessors, favoring naturalistic motifs and a combination of gemstones and precious metals.

Lucretia McMurtrie came from a wealthy Boston family and spent a few years of her childhood living in Paris. In 1900 she married Henry S. Bush and moved to Chestnut Hill. In 1911, a few years after her mother's

FIG. 30
Brooches are very versatile ornaments. Here, William McGregor Paxton portrays his mother wearing a black dress with an elaborate lace collar and a gold and turquoise brooch positioned at the neckline.

death, she sold her share of her family home on Marlborough Street in Boston's Back Bay to her sister Mary.[13] She had joined the Society of Arts and Crafts as a jeweler the previous year. It's unknown where she received her training, but she was so skilled that after just five years of membership she was elevated to the rank of Master.[14] Known examples of her work are extremely rare. One of them, a gold, turquoise, and pearl brooch, is quite similar to a design by Elizabeth Copeland. Made in 18-karat gold, it shows her refinement as a goldsmith (pl. 22).

The year that Bush became a master craftsperson, Gertrude Twichell joined the SAC. Twichell had studied with Laurin Hovey Martin and, like her instructor, is remembered primarily as an enamellist. Few examples of Twichell's jewelry survive, among them a large-scale brooch with a naturalistic shape of seven stylized peacock feathers, each with an oval citrine and purple, blue, and green enamel, which conveys the design harmony for which Twichell, and the Boston jewelers, were known (pl. 21). Yet its scale and fluidity set it apart from other contemporary ornaments. It has more in common with Shaw's oversized necklace than with the smaller works produced by craftspeople like Hale and Rogers.

Oakes put his own twist on the Boston jewelers' tradition of borrowing themes from nature by cleverly using his last name as an inspiration. His pieces, featuring leaves, especially oak leaves, and other natural forms, combine metalwork and gemstones in a way that builds on the examples of his teachers (pl. 14). Whereas Hale and Shaw usually made the gemstone the centerpiece, Oakes carefully considered the relationship between stone choice and metalwork and created designs where each cannot exist without the other. More dimensional than the work of his teachers, Oakes's jewelry incorporates radiant gemstones that appear as if sprinkled onto the design (pl. 15). After striking out on his own, Oakes remained in the good graces of both his mentors. In 1928, following a dinner party, Hale wrote a note to Oakes making it clear the two had maintained a social and professional relationship: "Your loyalty to me has always pleased and gratified me, and I am always proud of your beautiful jewelry which develops and grows every year."[15] In 1930, when Shaw retired, she directed all her commissions toward Oakes's studio.[16]

Oakes once claimed, "Springing from lapidaries as I do, the attraction with precious stones... is a matter of hereditary rather than an acquired taste."[17] With his meticulous attention to detail and great interest in gemstones, Oakes's jewels bear comparison to the work of Louis Comfort Tiffany, and indeed he was awarded a Tiffany Foundation Fellowship that allowed him to spend time at the artist's splendid 580-acre, 84-room Long Island estate, Laurelton Hall. Many brooches and necklaces from Tiffany Studios framed exceptional specimens with garland surrounds that highlighted the front and reverse of gemstones such as black opals (see fig. 41). Oakes, like Tiffany, believed that the back of the jewel must be as beautifully crafted as the front—and some of his necklaces were designed to be reversible, such as a cross with pearls on one side and amethyst on the other (pl. 16).[18] From Tiffany, Oakes learned to "do a little more work on the piece if necessary, but do it right," even if that meant that he took a loss in selling the work, or didn't sell it at all.[19] His aesthetic and dedication to his craft are evident in his entire oeuvre.

Oakes continued to work in the style he helped codify until his death in 1960, continuing to influence later jewelers through his own work and the education of students in annual workshops. Oakes passed the torch to his son Gilbert and then to his granddaughter Susan Oakes Peabody, who still maintains the Oakes Studio.[20] As a result, he is among the best remembered of the Boston jewelers.

While many members of Hale's circle worked in Boston and exhibited and sold their jewelry at the Society of Arts and Crafts, a good number of the metalworkers and jewelers who trained in the city settled elsewhere, helping to spread the Boston style to other parts of Massachusetts and across the country. Shaw relocated to Duxbury, and Oakes set up a summer studio in New Hampshire. Hale spent summers in Marblehead, Massachusetts. Jessie Ames Dunbar summered on Monhegan Island, while Hazel Blake French worked year-round on Cape Cod. After being educated in Boston, Mildred Watkins returned to Cleveland, to teach and work. The Society of Arts and Crafts also expanded its geographical reach in the 1920s, setting up an outpost at 721 Madison Avenue in New York City.[21]

The summer studios scattered around New England introduced vacationers to the jewelry being made in Boston. In 1916 Jessie Ames Dunbar was considered a leading art jeweler alongside Shaw, Hale, and Rogers; one author of an article on handwrought jewelry mentioned her work as having "special importance."[22] Dunbar divided her time between Boston—where after 1916 she worked alongside Margaret Rogers at 26 Lime Street—and rocky Monhegan Island, an artists' community ten miles off the coast of Maine. For decades Dunbar sold her jewelry on the island, in an eponymous studio-retail space (fig. 31).[23] In similar fashion, Oakes entertained clients and buyers in the White Mountains of New Hampshire. While Dunbar and Oakes spread the Boston look to the north, Hazel Blake French worked to the south of Boston. In 1914 she set up a year-round studio in Sandwich.[24] The location, in the heart of Cape Cod, was well placed to attract beach-going vacationers. French worked in silver and glass, in place of gemstones. The Boston and Sandwich Glass Company had closed in 1888, two years before she was born, and since her childhood French had combed the area around the former factory for fragments of colored glass. French would send these bits of rubble to a New York lapidary for cutting and polishing and then used them like gemstones in her jewelry.[25] Among her peers, she was the only one who consistently worked in alternative materials, and she

FIG. 31
During the summer months Jessie Ames Dunbar ran a studio-shop on Monhegan Island, off the coast of Maine. This photograph of Dunbar taken around 1920 shows her sitting by a table with her jewelry laid out on it.

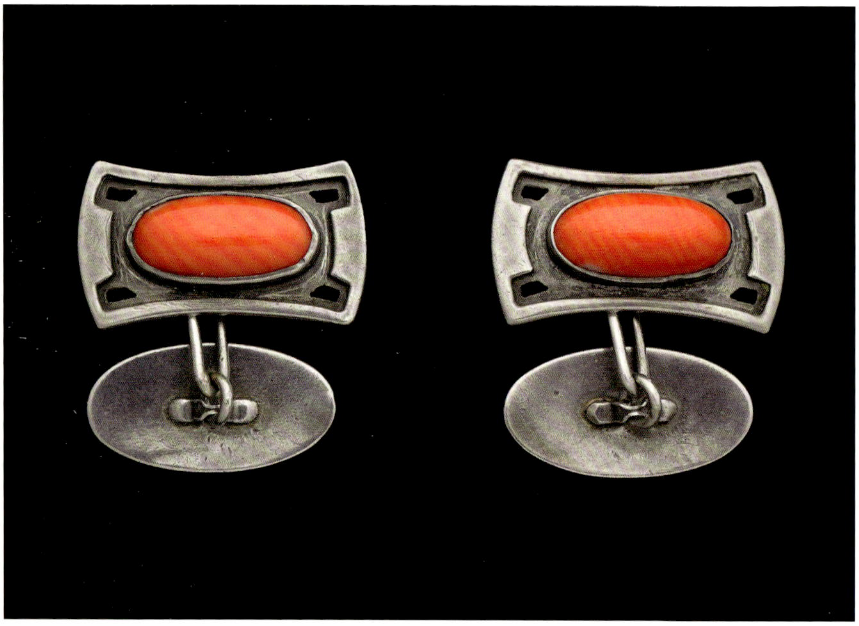

FIG. 32
Boston and Chicago were both major centers of Arts and Crafts jewelry, with subtle distinctions between the two cities' styles. Chicago jewelers such as the Kalo Shop preferred humbler materials than those used in Boston, as in these coral and silver cufflinks.

was the first member of the Society of Arts and Crafts allowed to exhibit faux gemstones.

By the 1920s, Boston had established itself as an artistic center, and had codified a style that included precious metals and a mix of cabochon and faceted gemstones. Aside from Boston, the other important center for jewelry making in the United States was Chicago, which led the development of regional styles throughout the Midwest during the early decades of the twentieth century.[26] Chicago jewels typically featured a single center stone with a metalwork surround, often in silver (fig. 32). Jewelers who trained in Boston and then settled elsewhere, as Mildred Watkins did, helped to disseminate the Boston style more broadly, but they may have also caused confusion about its identity. As jewelers continued to develop outside Boston, the style evolved. In Boston, the look remained consistent into the middle of the twentieth century, as Oakes continued to retail his work at the Society of Arts and Crafts showroom in the 1950s.

GALLERY

PLATES 12 AND 13
Integrating design and fabrication skills, Josephine Hartwell Shaw brings materials to the forefront in these two long statement necklaces. Both incorporate found objects—carved white jade from China on the left, and carved tourmaline and rose quartz on the right.

PLATE 14

All of the Boston jewelers made pieces whose design included leaves or flower blossoms. Edward Everett Oakes sometimes played on his last name by featuring oak

PLATE 15
This circle pin shows how Oakes integrated design and materials, sprinkling diamond and pearls into the metalwork to become an essential element in the design.

PLATE 16
Oakes often commented that the refinement of a jewel's reverse was as important to him as the execution of the front. This reversible necklace with a cross pendant features pearls on one side and amethysts on the other.

PLATE 17

Color was one element that defined the Boston look. In this pink and purple cross pendant, Shaw has combined pearls, amethysts, and rose quartz.

PLATE 18
Cabochon-cut chrysoprase and pearls with gold floral surrounds alternate in this necklace by Margaret Rogers. The short-style necklace was a form that Rogers often repeated, using different colors of gemstones and natural motifs in metal.

PLATE 19
Rogers combined polychrome gemstones in innovative ways. The gems shine, as the metalwork disappears into the background, in a brooch featuring a central opal surrounded by pearl, citrine, and pink sapphire.

PLATE 20
This brooch by Elizabeth Copeland, with a turquoise in a floral-garlanded gold frame and a small opal drop, is strikingly similar to the one worn by Paxton's mother, Rose, in her portrait.

PLATE 21
Because of their fragility, examples of enamel jewelry are rare. Gertrude Twichell combines blue, green, and purple enamel with oval citrine "eyes" in the peacock feathers in this large ornament.

PLATE 22
This rare example of Lucretia Bush's work shows her refinement as a goldsmith. Like Copeland's brooch (pl. 20), the design also frames turquoise in gold, and adds pearls to the ornamental metalwork.

PLATES 23 AND 24
Two brooches by Jessie Ames Dunbar include a kaleidoscope of cabochon and faceted gems that range from orange, pink, and blue sapphires to red, green, and watermelon tourmalines.

PLATE 25
Hazel Blake French carefully selected glass from the rubble of the Sandwich Glass Company, had it cut and polished, and set it like gemstones, as in this silver necklace.

CONSUMING ARTS AND CRAFTS

Emily Stoehrer

Who was wearing Boston Arts and Crafts jewelry, and what forms of dress were they wearing it with? Descriptions of the jewels as they were worn are rare; one of the few comes from Elizabeth Stone, who imaginatively declared that "the jewelry carried with it visions of wearers never less than six foot two, moving with a theatrical impermeability to the fixed gaze of their fellow creatures."[1] It's true that some of the necklaces were extraordinarily long—for example, the butterfly pendant on one necklace by Frank Gardner Hale would have fallen into the wearer's lap when she was seated (fig. 33; see pl. 26). Some have suggested that dress reformers—who sought to improve women's health and ease movement by promoting less restrictive garments—would have been the primary consumers of Arts and Crafts jewelry. But although the dress reform movement had been active in Boston in the 1870s, by 1900 women's fashions had adopted a more modern tailored silhouette for daywear.[2] It's more likely that the wearer of this jewelry was a patron of the arts who wore her handwrought, locally made jewelry with the fashionable dress styles of the day. Enthusiasts in Boston would have encountered artist-made jewelry at exhibitions of the Society of Arts and Crafts, but the jewelers also gained a national following after they participated in the Louisiana Purchase Exposition in 1904, and newspapers and popular magazines regularly reported on the work of Hale and his contemporaries.

From early on, the Society of Arts and Crafts was committed to providing patrons with the opportunity to purchase jewelry made by its members. On December 8, 1900, the organization opened its initial permanent retail operation at 14 Somerset Street, near the top of Beacon Hill. It was run by Fredrick A. Whiting, the Society's first paid employee. The third--floor salesroom, which shared space with the Society's offices, was open to the public daily from 11 am to 2 pm. Two years later they settled at 9 Park Street, in a more prominent location near the State House and the Boston Common. The new shop had street-level windows that drew a greater number of visitors, helping to boost sales almost tenfold and increasing membership in and recognition of the SAC. The Annual Report for 1904 boasted: "A frequent visitor during the past year recently went to the New York store of a jewelry company of international reputation and was conscious of a keen regret that their work had deteriorated so greatly in a year—finally realizing that she was judging their factory productions by the standard unconsciously absorbed during her visits to our rooms since she was last in New York."[3]

In 1908, in response to requests from the SAC's Metal Worker's Guild, the shop's displays were rearranged, lighting was improved, staff salaries were increased, bookkeeping was modified, and a special case was added for exhibits of work by individual artists. The six-foot-long case was available to members to rent for three dollars per week, an opportunity quickly grasped by the jewelers who could afford it, including Josephine Hartwell Shaw.[4] In 1912 the salesroom was again enlarged and renovated, and the entire rear gallery was offered to individual members or small groups for exhibition at fifteen dollars per week, with the requirement that all objects were still to be vetted by the SAC Jury.[5] An additional jewelry case was installed in the summer of 1913, "as there is now gold jewelry enough to require a case to itself."[6]

The Park Street location remained the shop's home until 1930, when it relocated to Newbury Street. Expanding its presence, the Society operated a second retail showroom on Manhattan's Upper East Side —The Arts & Crafts Shop—during the 1920s.[7] The shops offered artists an outlet for their work and gave consumers a year-round venue for viewing and purchasing pieces by the Society's members. These showrooms catered to local patrons and visitors alike. Front-page advertisements in city shopping guides, such as in a weekly Boston pamphlet from 1928, alerted visitors to the city to the existence of the showroom and illustrated the type of jewelry sold there (fig. 34). Meanwhile, inclusion of the jewelers' work in national expositions and on the lecture circuit brought jewelers in contact with a geographically diverse audience.

FIG. 33
It's rare to find an example of Boston jewelry in its original box. This monumental necklace, with its oversized pendant and extraordinarily long chain, is custom fitted into the box's brown and gold brocaded interior. The words "Frank Gardner Hale" and "Boston" are embossed in gold on the left side.

While retail records and annual reports offer evidence of vibrant sales, there remain few written accounts of the style choices of Boston women, but depictions by contemporary Boston painters offer a wealth of information on the city residents' fashion preferences. When these paintings are considered alongside national fashion magazines like *Vogue* and *Harper's Bazaar*, which chronicled high-style American fashion, and decorative arts publications like *House Beautiful*, which discussed work by artist-craftspeople, including jewelers, a picture begins to emerge of the clothing that accompanied this jewelry.

FIG. 34
By the 1920s Boston's Society of Arts and Crafts was in the vanguard of locally made jewelry. The cover of a weekly shopping guide features a photograph of two necklaces and a brooch. The lower necklace, in silver and lapis lazuli from Russia, is by Hale (see pl. 27).

FIG. 35
Paintings by William Paxton, like *The New Necklace* (1910), celebrate the tastes of the era and feature sumptuous decorative arts. The two fashionable figures seen here are the type of patron that Boston jewelers catered to.

William Paxton's painting *The New Necklace* offers a glimpse inside the home of a Boston woman in 1910 (fig. 35). The intimate scene was likely staged in the artist's studio, but the sumptuous clothing, period furniture, and decorative arts illustrate the era's interest in Asian art as well as taste for lavishly decorated interiors. A standing figure dressed in a green day dress places a gold necklace in the palm of a seated woman. The recipient, who seems to have been interrupted while writing a letter, is depicted wearing a Chinese jacket over a pink taffeta petticoat. Similar clothing styles appear in the fashion press of the time, and it's quite likely that a tasteful, artistic consumer of Boston Arts and Crafts jewelry may have presented herself like either of these two women. Jewelry by Hale, Shaw, or Rogers would have paired well with a dress such as the one worn by the standing figure.

Although most of the jewelry that Paxton included in his paintings is traditional, he depicted a turquoise-colored brooch that resembles one by Elizabeth Copeland in a portrait of his mother (see fig. 30) and again, worn by his wife, in *The Crystal* (fig. 36; compare pl. 20). An instructor at the School of the Museum of Fine Arts, Paxton would have been familiar with the city's blossoming jewelry and metalworking scene. He used jewelry—scattered across a dressing table, fingered by a sitter as she gazes at the artist, or adding a pop of color to an ensemble—to aid in his creation of a mise-en-scène that illustrates how dress and ornament complemented each other.[8]

PAXTON
1910

The few known early consumers of Arts and Crafts jewels were patrons of the arts or artists themselves, as well as fashionable women. The stage actress Julia Marlowe was a supporter of the city's Arts and Crafts metalsmiths and an active feminist (fig. 37).[9] Her tastes in jewelry were noted in an industry magazine, *The Jeweler's Review*, in 1899, when the Massachusetts manufacturer's jeweler R. F. Simmons & Co. named a bracelet design after her.[10] While her name surely helped drive sales for the mass-produced bracelet, Marlowe came to prefer designer-crafted jewelry. In 1916, an article in *The International Studio* reported that Marlowe—who at five feet six inches was not quite the towering presence imagined by Elizabeth Stone—commissioned some of Josephine Shaw's most exemplary work.[11] She also had numerous pieces made by the Boston silversmith Arthur Stone, Elizabeth's husband, from 1911 to the 1920s.[12]

The *International Studio* article additionally featured a dramatic moonstone and platinum collar with a long pendant that belonged to a prominent

FIG. 36
In *The Crystal* Paxton depicts his wife, Elizabeth Oakie, seated and wearing a yellow evening dress while contemplating a translucent orb. Pinned to her sleeve is a brooch quite similar to the one seen in the portrait of Paxton's mother (see fig. 30), and on her right hand is a matching turquoise ring.

FIG. 37
The stage actress Julia Marlowe was among Josephine Shaw's clients. In this photograph by Frances Johnston from the early years of the twentieth century, Marlowe isn't wearing any jewelry, but her daytime ensemble is of the type described by Hale and by journalists as being particularly well-suited for colorful cabochon ornaments.

Bostonian, Mrs. Eben D. Jordan, whose father-in-law had founded the Jordan Marsh department store chain.[13] May S. Jordan, born in 1861, lived in a mansion in Brookline before moving to her husband's family home at 46 Beacon Street, not far from the SAC showroom on Park Street, in Boston around 1897.[14] She was an art collector and patron of the arts who would naturally have been interested in artist-made jewelry. The moonstone necklace illustrated in the magazine article had been displayed in 1911, alongside a selection of jewelry by Shaw that was owned by a Mrs. Fitch Gilbert of Cambridge, at an exhibition at the Museum of Fine Arts, Boston.[15]

In the first decades of the twentieth century, as clothing became simpler, jewelry and accessories gained importance. In 1908, silver and jewelry made up more than a fifth of the SAC showroom sales, and jewelry received the highest accolades from the Society's jury.[16] That same year, Josephine Shaw told the *Boston Daily Globe*, "A woman's taste in dress counts for much, but it is the jewelry she affects that at once reveals her individuality, her refinement and her culture, or her lack of it."[17] The staged paintings by Paxton may not reflect their subjects' individual taste in jewelry, but they do offer a rare glimpse at how an ornament might have been worn. Brooches were the most versatile of ornaments and, as Paxton demonstrates, early twentieth-century women wore them in creative ways at the collar of a dress or even on a sleeve.

Shaw's remarks imply, and contemporary etiquette books confirm, that jewelry could look vulgar if worn inappropriately. As jewelry became more readily available at a wide variety of price points, fashion periodicals increasingly addressed matters of taste. Women in Boston had a choice of retailers at all levels. The city boasted many fine jewelry establishments, including Maynard & Potter, on Boylston Street; Bigelow, Kennard & Co., on the corner of West and Washington Streets; and Shreve, Crump & Low, on Tremont Street near the Boston Common. Nearby, at 1 Summer Street, the Jordan Marsh department store sold fashion-focused jewelry, much of it made in Providence, Rhode Island, by manufacturers like Ostby & Barton, in its first-floor showrooms.[18] In contrast, the artistic jewelry sold by the Society of Arts and Crafts offered one-of-a-kind pieces, and its many offerings by female jewelers would have appealed to women seeking tasteful yet fashionable ornaments.

Because jewelry lasted longer than clothing and represented more of an investment, its design had traditionally been less influenced by ephemeral trends. The introduction of costume jewelry offered an inexpensive way for jewelry to reflect the latest fashions. As artist-jewelers grappled with this new, more affordable, and ever-changing style of jewelry, readers of *House Beautiful* were encouraged to think about jewelry as an heirloom. Ralph Bergengren wrote of Josephine Shaw's jewels: "Leave 'milady' her 'bijouterie,' deciding for her whether she is tall enough to wear the 'intricate, Oriental things' or 'delicately fashioned' enough for the 'fragile, tranquil ones,' or 'massive' enough... and leave Mrs. Shaw, down there in the country, making jewels with the primary ambition to create something that will still be preserved for its own worth long after the most 'massive' and the most 'delicately fashioned' of her contemporaries shall be crumbled to dust altogether."[19] During the 1920s the Society of Arts and Crafts also encouraged consumers to think about jewelry as potential heirlooms. Simultaneously, jewelers were sensitive to the shift and adapted their narrative with fashion in mind.

Ostby & Barton first used the phrase "costume jewelry" in 1916, in a full-page advertisement that ran in *Harper's Bazaar* and *Vogue*.[20] The didactic text claims that interest in costume jewelry emerged in Paris, where fashionable women wanted ornaments that complemented their ensembles. The jewelry illustrated in the ad was described as being designed by artists; it was made of 14-karat yellow or white gold and included "reproductions" of precious gemstones as well as rhinestones and enamel. The concern that commercial firms would make inexpensive copies of artist-designed pieces led some Arts and Crafts jewelers to bar visitors from their workshop. In a newspaper interview from 1908, the New York jeweler Edith Vail recalled how a local manufacture stole her designs after illicitly gaining entry to her studio.[21] Both jewelers and journalists grumbled about the "sameness" of mass-produced ornaments and celebrated the artistry and handcraftsmanship of fine jewelry.[22] As jewelry became accessible to more buyers, individual jewelry makers recognized the importance of aligning their products with current fashion, and some retailers began to see the value in artist-made options. In April 1922, a gallery on Fifth Avenue in New York announced that it was selling earrings and "costume jewelry" by Frank Gardner Hale.[23]

In an article comparing the jewelry of New York's high society to the manufactured and Arts and Crafts jewelry of the day, the author commented that "it cannot be so delicate that it will not wear well, or the very idea of jewelry is lost; it is primarily intended to be worn."[24] This advice was not lost on Boston jewelers: in writings and lectures, both Hale and Edward Everett Oakes advised consumers on appropriate ways to wear jewels. Hale stated, "I consider it very good taste for women to wear jewelry, but I don't need to tell you there is a time and a place for it, and no woman should play tennis or golf, wearing a diamond bar pin or a sunburst—the jewelry worn should be of such a nature as will look well on sports clothes." He went on to encourage a "simple pin or clip" in gold or silver, "leaving the more precious metal for afternoon or evening use."[25] Oakes encouraged women to own a variety of rings, but cautioned them against the trend of "wearing several diamond rings on one hand" and advocated sporting "one ring on a hand at one time, appropriate size for the hand[,] which is smart and attractive."[26]

During the early twentieth century, women of a certain status would have changed clothes multiple times a day, with dresses becoming more sumptuous and more revealing as the day progressed.[27] A skirt and blouse were worn in the morning, day dresses were long and modestly cut, and afternoon dresses were made with higher quality fabrics and trimmings. Evenings were reserved for the most luxurious dresses, worn with platinum and diamond jewelry. Hale confirmed that colorful cabochon-cut gemstones, unlikely to be worn in the evening, would be "very appropriate for day use."[28]

An article in *Good Housekeeping* magazine in 1911 observed, "The changes in costume are studied by the designers of jewelry, and have more or less influence on their work." The author went on to instruct women to wear a ring and earrings in the morning, and a watch or simple bracelet during the day (fig. 38). She referred to Arts and Crafts jewelry as "tailored jewelry"—describing it as handwrought jewelry in silver or gold, with semiprecious gemstones—and illustrated pieces by Josephine Shaw and Margaret Rogers. This jewelry was recommended as pairing well with the "informal costume of the street," such as a shirtwaist and skirt, tailored frock, or suit, and was suggested for "informal occasions."[29] Accessories like belt buckles, bar brooches, and circle pins would have complemented daytime dresses, with the more spectacular Arts and Crafts necklaces reserved for afternoon attire.

By 1920 Hale and his contemporaries had codified the Boston look, but fashions were about to change drastically during the coming decade. As clothing became more streamlined and hemlines inched shorter, a different style of jewelry was required. Earrings were one type of ornament that producers and consumers both struggled to adopt. By 1911 stud earrings had been replaced by long pendant earrings, and by the 1920s even the most conservative jewelers could not omit earrings from their offerings.[30] Hale complained that "ear-rings are the only ornaments retained by civilized nations which necessitate a mutation of the body before they can be worn." However, after initially resisting the wearing of earrings as a passing fad, he

eventually "fell victim to the craze."[31] Fashion magazines associated interest in longer earrings with the decade's adoption of shorter hairstyles, like the bob.[32] Hale tried to encourage his contemporaries to follow the whims of fashion, declaring, "The craftsman's technique changes, and even his taste *should*, for one must follow fashions, and to a degree, fads, in order to produce things acceptable to modern times and fashions."[33] Nonetheless, many jewelers struggled to keep up with the ever-changing fashions in dress and hairstyles, and by the late 1920s the popularity of Boston jewelry had dwindled.

FIG. 38
In 1911, *Good Housekeeping* instructed readers that "a simple bracelet" was appropriate for the daytime. Despite its costly materials, this gold, platinum, diamond, and ruby example—made by Oakes some years later—is of the style described.

One of the most fashion-forward designs to come out of Boston during the twenties was a gold tassel by Oakes (pl. 43). He made at least three related pendants, one of which—a gold, pearl, and sapphire tassel on a silk cord—was purchased by the Metropolitan Museum of Art in 1923. In the other examples, the tassel is suspended from a long gold chain. Oakes's necklace is a good example of a piece that is at once a costume jewel and an heirloom, well suited to *la mode* but of such good design and execution that it was acquired by the country's leading fine art museum. During the 1920s most Boston jewelers continued making jewelry in the established Arts and

Crafts style, and *Vogue* told its readers in 1921 that "colorful semi-precious jewelry is encouraged as a way to compliment the increasingly black ensembles."[34] In a show of refreshing stylistic diversity, Oakes—unlike many of his peers—attempted to adopt a more geometric, Art Deco aesthetic in the tassel necklace, as well as in a gold brooch with sapphires and diamonds and an extraordinary jeweled casket (see figs. 39, 40).

With rare exceptions, though, tradition reigned in Boston. The look that had been pioneered in the early years of the twentieth century continued to be employed during the 1920s, as the community of jewelry makers largely resisted change. The achievements of the Arts and Crafts jewelers were recognized when the Museum of Fine Arts, Boston, acquired pieces by Copeland and Shaw, and the Metropolitan Museum acquired work by Oakes. In the late 1920s, SAC advertisements encouraged shoppers to think about their jewelry as being museum quality. But at the end of the decade, Hale would lament that Boston jewelers had "made an enviable place for ourselves, and then came the market crash."[35]

Hale was correct in identifying the stock market crash as the end of the heyday of Boston jewelry. By considering the paintings and periodicals made during this brief moment in the city's history, we can begin to imagine the fashionable world of early twentieth-century Boston, but much remains to be learned about the women who purchased and wore this jewelry. The few surviving sale records confirm that patrons of Arts and Crafts jewelers were geographically dispersed—with many customers from New England, but also buyers in New York, Ohio, and Texas. The jewelry appealed to an engaged consumer who not only shopped in the Society of Arts and Crafts showrooms but also read magazines that published articles on its craftspeople. As Oakes put it, "the purchaser is very interested in the artist," making it likely that some buyers sought out jewelers and developed relationships with them.[36] Alongside craftspeople, such patrons participated in the local arts community, attended expositions and lectures, and visited summer studios, where they had more direct access to the jewelers. The consumers and wearers of Arts and Crafts jewelry in Boston helped shape its development and bring national attention to the creations of its makers.

GALLERY

PLATE 26
Among the longest and most dramatic of the known examples by Boston jewelers, this necklace by Frank Gardner Hale features a large butterfly pendant with carved jade wings, a blue-green enamel body, and gold antennae.

PLATE 27
Featured on the cover of the city's shopping guide in 1928 (see fig. 34), this silver and carved lapis lazuli necklace by Hale demonstrates his artistic range of materials and design styles.

PLATE 28
A gold, pearl, and emerald ring is one of the few known designs by Josephine Hartwell Shaw. It was acquired by the Museum of Fine Arts, Boston, along with a small square gold and pearl brooch (see fig. 10), in 1913.

PLATE 29
While platinum and diamond rings were reserved for more formal evening occasions, colorful rings like this sapphire, diamond, and pearl example by Margaret Rogers were encouraged for daytime wear.

PLATE 30
Hale tried to avoid the "craze" for earrings, but this silver and carved carnelian pair demonstrate that his resistance was futile. As hairstyles became shorter, fashion magazines encouraged the wearing of longer earrings, and eventually even the Boston jewelers succumbed to the trend.

PLATE 31

During the early twentieth century, daytime fashions included a shirtwaist bodice and skirt, often worn with a belt and buckle at the waist. Elaborate ornaments, like this silver and enamel belt buckle with a design of galleon ships by Hale, were created to add color and individuality to the otherwise uniform style of dress.

PLATES 32 AND 33

Brooches added a personal flair to daytime clothing and could be positioned to adorn a neckline, sleeve, or waistline. Hale sometimes used unusual gemstones in his jewelry—the light green gem in the brooch at top is a tourmaline, and the orange centerpiece in the one below is a carnelian intaglio with a coat of arms.

PLATES 34–37
Over the course of Edward Everett Oakes's long career, he made many brooches in a wide variety of forms and materials. The horizontal bar brooch and the circle pin dominate, but he also designed more inventive pieces, like this large curved brooch with gold leaves and diamond and sapphire blossoms.

PLATES 38 AND 39
Hale selected amethysts to evoke the color of what he is depicting in silver. In these two examples, the purple gems complement grapevine and thistle motifs.

PLATE 40
Unlike her peers, who nearly always included scrolling vines and leaves in their metalwork, here Rogers uses the bezel and surround to create a metal blossom around her colored gemstones.

PLATE 41
Illustrated by a photograph in *Good Housekeeping* in 1911, this silver, amethyst, aquamarine, and pearl "sea-weed motif necklace" was described as an example of "The New Jewelry Art." The accompanying article carefully outlines how to wear this jewelry with the latest fashions.

PLATE 42
In this silver, gold, and pearl necklace by Shaw, each pearl is a different size and shape. Unusual, oddly shaped, or colored pearls were favored by Arts and Crafts jewelers.

PLATE 43
This gold and agate design by Oakes is among the most fashion-forward designs created by a Boston jeweler. Favored for their movement, tassels were a popular element in necklaces during the 1920s.

LEGACY AND INFLUENCE

Nonie Gadsden

On October 17, 1929, Hale's protégé Edward Everett Oakes unveiled his self-proclaimed "masterpiece" in the showrooms of the Society of Arts and Crafts. The jewel-encrusted silver casket (or jewelry box) fulfilled his "dream of leaving some single magnificent work which will compare favorably with the heritage from the great jewelers of the Renaissance."[1] Its architectural form is ornamented with the delicate, foliate motifs that Oakes had adapted from Hale, as well as more modern elements such as the stepped, skyscraper-like arrangement of rectangular jewels at the box's corners (fig. 39). Oakes had spent three years conceiving and designing this work, and gathering its expensive materials, including 143 carefully matched purple amethysts, 86 Japanese pearls, and 88 black onyx stones, sourced from as far away as Siberia, Asia, and South America. The result of his painstaking labor was immediately lauded by Boston critics as a tour de force of both craftsmanship and design. Oakes's hope that the Museum of Fine Arts would acquire his masterwork was dashed just days after its initial presentation, when the stock market crash touched off an economic depression that would last nearly a decade. The jeweled casket remained in the Oakes family for more than seventy years before it was finally acquired by the MFA.

As the story of Edward Everett Oakes's ill-fated masterpiece illustrates, the fortunes of Arts and Crafts jewelry plummeted along with the stock market. Although the movement had steadily lost favor in popular U.S. culture since World War I, it remained prominent in New England through the

1920s. Boston's intellectual leadership in defining Arts and Crafts ideals had so ingrained the superiority of handicrafts that machine age aesthetics were particularly slow to take hold among New England's cultured elite. In Boston, Arts and Crafts jewelry retained a devoted following of makers and consumers despite the national resurgence of ostentatious high-style jewelry in modern designs accompanied by the growth of mass-manufactured inexpensive costume jewelry. Some jewelers, like Oakes, incorporated modernist motifs in their work to keep up with current styles. For example, an Oakes circle brooch likely made in the late 1920s incorporates Art Deco–inspired geometric columns of faceted sapphires to contrast with the more flowing Arts and Crafts floral motifs (fig. 40). Other craftspeople, such as Hale, dug in their heels and clung to a more conservative look. The Great Depression severely curtailed the market for all independent craftspeople, especially those working in luxury crafts such as jewelry. Although a few Arts and Crafts jewelry makers were able to weather the storm—for instance, Oakes turned to making stock-design wedding and engagement rings—many abandoned their craft. Yet the influence of Hale, Oakes, and their Boston contemporaries on jewelry making in the United States, widespread during their lifetimes, endures to this day.

In their own time, Boston's jewelry makers were pioneers and national leaders, through their individual actions and their participation in the Society of Arts and Crafts. They mentored jewelry makers in their studios, in schools, in lectures and writings, and through their service on the SAC Jury. They promoted the Arts and Crafts philosophy and developed a market for their creations through exhibitions, competitions, and sales. And they restored the dignity of handcraftsmanship and revitalized older craft techniques. But it is hard to say definitively that Boston's jewelry makers were the inventors of the style they championed and disseminated.

The origins of a style can be hard to pin down in the modernizing world of the early twentieth century, where objects traveled the globe for international exhibitions, and images and information circulated quickly through trade and popular magazines. The jewelry made in Boston is distinctive; compared to Arts and Crafts ornaments made in England, for example, it

FIG. 39
The interior of Edward Everett Oakes's jewel-encrusted silver casket is as beautifully finished as the exterior; it offers a shallow, velvet-lined removable tray above a larger lower compartment. The casket rests on a custom carved laurel-wood stand, also made by Oakes.

FIG. 40
This gold, sapphire, and diamond brooch made in the 1920s by Oakes shows the influence of the geometric Art Deco style.

is more stylized, thinner and more delicate, and, for lack of a better word, more restrained. Jewelry makers in Boston embraced the French Art Nouveau practice of using gold more than most of their counterparts in England did, so the more expensive material may explain the thinner lines of the mounts. However, at the same time, craftspeople elsewhere in the United States, most notably James Winn and Florence Koehler in Chicago and Louis Comfort Tiffany in New York, worked in styles similar to those seen in Boston. Where did this American look originate?

The striking resemblance between one of Hale's necklace designs and a finished work designed by Louis Comfort Tiffany illustrates the difficulty of teasing out an answer (fig. 41). Both works focus on a single black opal, chosen for color and beauty rather than monetary value; both stones are mounted in delicate gold wires sculpted to look like grapevines; and both hang from an intricate multi-strand chain whose ornament echoes the colors and textures of the pendant, creating a harmonious whole. Tiffany's necklace—like most of Hale's work, and that of many of his Boston contemporaries—is finished on the back as well as the front, in a display of craftsmanship and artistry (fig. 42). Yet the personal aesthetic of each designer is still evident: Hale's vines tend to be orderly and stylized, while Tiffany's are more fluid and dynamic. Although the necklaces by Hale and Tiffany bear a striking resemblance, it remains unclear if one influenced the other. While it is difficult to pin down the precise origin of this style, Boston's artist jewelers, guided by the SAC Jury, embraced and championed it, making it their own.

Following the early leadership of Boston's artist jewelers and the authority of the Boston Society of Arts and Crafts, jewelry makers across the country came to embrace the Boston look of delicate and restrained vegetal designs in gold and silver with boldly colored gemstones or enamel. With

FIG. 41
A design drawing for a pendant necklace by Frank Gardner Hale uses pencil to outline the shapes and watercolor to simulate the variegated colors of the stones and enamels.

FIG. 42
Louis Comfort Tiffany highlighted the natural properties of this extraordinary black opal with sinuous gold leaves and vines that resemble the stone's matrix and circular-cut green demantoid garnets and blue sapphires that echo the stone's colors. The sculpted gold metalwork on the back of the pendant is even more impressive than that on the front.

time, what was once an avant-garde regional style transformed into a conservative national style.

Many artists who trained under Boston's Arts and Crafts leaders initially created work that imitated their teachers, and then went on to apply their skills to exploring new styles. The Missouri-born jewelry maker Margret Craver (1907–2010) came of age in the early 1930s, just after Arts and Crafts jewelry fell from favor and many of the metal training programs established at the beginning of the century had shifted their focus to industrial design. Craver patched together a series of independent short-term training opportunities from a range of American metalworkers, including a conservator of arms and armor at the Metropolitan Museum of Art, a commercial silversmith at Tiffany & Co., and the workshop of Arthur Stone, the prominent Arts and Crafts silversmith, in Gardner, Massachusetts. One of her early works is a silver necklace made around 1935 that features a large yellow sapphire encased in a tangle of leafy vines accented with green tourmalines, all hanging from a double chain embellished with smaller leaf and tourmaline clusters (fig. 43). The influence of the earlier Boston craftsmen in the ornament's overall design, details, and technique is unmistakable. With time and further study in Sweden, Craver's style evolved to a more modern look. Yet she continued to live by an Arts and Crafts ethos: during World War II, she initiated and developed a therapeutic metalsmithing program in military hospitals for wounded veterans, using art and handcrafts to improve lives. And in the 1950s, shortly after moving to the Boston area, Craver dedicated herself to rediscovering the challenging seventeenth-century technique of *émail en résille sur verre* (enamel in a network on glass), in which a design is etched in glass, then lined with gold foil and the hollow filled with translucent enamel. The result of this technique, as seen in Craver's *Time* neck pendant, made about 1963, is a delicate floating design with a strong illusion of depth (fig. 44).[2] Craver followed in the footsteps of her Arts and Crafts predecessors by emphasizing the importance of handwork and pursuing her interest in resurrecting ancient craft techniques, yet she struck out on her own in a more modern style.

The leadership of Boston's Arts and Crafts artisans in the resurgence of enameling in the United States is similar to their role in codifying and disseminating the Boston style. Whereas British craftsmen such as Alexander Fisher deserve acknowledgment for reviving the techniques of Renaissance-era enameling, Boston artisans can be credited with popularizing the technique in the United States, with Laurin Hovey Martin and Frank Gardner Hale at the forefront. Martin taught enameling to scores of students and

FIG. 43
Margret Craver's necklace from the mid-1930s illustrates the lasting influence of the work of Hale and his Boston Arts and Crafts contemporaries.

published an instructional treatise on the technique in the magazine *Keramic Studio* in 1905. As early as 1907–8, Hale sought to elevate the status of the medium by exhibiting his small enamel plaques framed like paintings. A pictorial plaque featuring a shimmering underwater scene retains its original velvet-lined frame, bearing an exhibition sticker from the Society of Arts and Crafts (fig. 45). Hale's enamel work was exhibited and sold throughout the country; one plaque that he showed at the Speed Museum in Louisville, Kentucky, in February 1929 was purchased directly out of the exhibition for $55 by Mrs. Hattie Bishop Speed herself and remains in the museum's collection today.[3]

Two of Martin's pupils, Mildred G. Watkins and Kenneth F. Bates, used the skills they saw and learned in Boston to help develop an innovative community of art enamellists in Cleveland, Ohio.[4] Watkins (1883–1968) graduated from the Cleveland School of Art in 1901 with the ambition to become a metalsmith. She sought out training in Boston, studying silversmithing with George C. Gebelein and enameling with Martin, before returning to her native city and teaching at her alma mater from 1919 to 1953. Watkins's

FIG. 44
This gold necklace illustrates Craver's lifelong dedication to handwork and interest in materials; the pendant is composed of *émail en résille sur verre* (enamel in a network on glass), a lost seventeenth-century technique that Craver revived.

FIG. 45
An enamel plaque by Hale retains its original velvet-lined frame with a Society of Arts and Crafts sticker on the back.

early silver brooches reflect her Arts and Crafts training in Boston (figs. 46 and 47). These works incorporate enamel panels as a contained, decorative element subordinate to the overall design. As her style evolved, the enamel increasingly took precedence over the metalwork, making colorful images the focal point of her creations.

In 1927, Watkins likely helped to recruit Kenneth Bates (1904–1994), a promising student of her former mentor Laurin Hovey Martin, to join her as an instructor at the Cleveland School of Art.[5] Bates devoted his entire career to the art of enameling, ultimately being dubbed the "Dean of American Enamellists" by *Ceramics Monthly* in 1967. He used the foundational skills he learned from Martin to experiment with techniques, materials, and designs, pushing the boundaries of the field.[6] A dish Bates made in 1957, along with its design drawing, reveals his careful planning of works and his lifelong interest in color, in the context of a foray into modern abstraction (figs. 48 and 49). The title of the work, *Textures*, directs attention to the physical properties of enameling—and the act of titling the piece also aligns Bates's work with that of painters and sculptors, like Hale's framing of his work half a century earlier. Through Watkins, Bates, and others, the influence of Martin, Hale, and Boston's pioneering enamellers in the United States continued for decades after the end of their careers.

Yet the most enduring legacy of Boston Arts and Crafts jewelry makers manifested not in a specific style or technique, but in ideology and practice. By blazing a path whereby individual craftsmen could support themselves through the creation of handwrought jewelry and small enamels, Hale and his contemporaries laid the foundation for studio jewelry makers later in the century. Studio jewelry emerged after World War II as part of the broader studio craft movement, which arose in reaction to the monotony of mass-produced wares that dominated the midcentury marketplace. Like their Arts and Crafts predecessors, studio jewelers championed individual makers working alone or in small workshops and making one-of-a-kind products. Both movements incorporated precious and nonprecious materi-

FIGS. 46 AND 47
Two silver brooches by Mildred Watkins show her early enameling skill. The bar brooch with a central green chalcedony stone uses champlevé enameling, in which a cavity in the metal is filled with blue and green enamel swirled to resemble a peacock feather. In the octagonal brooch the surface below the turquoise enamel is carved with lines to give it texture and depth.

FIG. 48
The abstracted vegetal motifs of Kenneth Bates's tray harmonize with the enameled design motifs.

FIG. 49
Bates conducted extensive planning for his major works in enamel, including preliminary drawings, color renderings, and sample firings to test colors and mixtures. An ink and watercolor study in shades of black, brown, gray, and white shows the process of developing the shapes contained in the colorful final product.

als into their creations, emphasized design over intrinsic value, and strove to distinguish themselves from the commercial jewelry industry.

Unlike Arts and Crafts makers, however, most studio jewelers did not subscribe to a larger social or lifestyle reform philosophy, thus freeing themselves of the moralistic constraints imposed on their predecessors. Studio jewelers saw themselves as modern artists forging into the future, and marketed their wares using the model of the art world, rather than those of fashion or retailing.[7] Studio jewelry makers favored originality of design and concept over historical revivals, producing jewelry in a tremendous variety of styles. Many followed trends in the contemporary art world, and some even elevated concept over craftsmanship or wearability.

The ongoing influence of Hale and his contemporaries was especially lasting within the studio jewelry community in Boston. Miyé Matsukata (1922–1981), a studio jewelry maker based in the city, followed in the footsteps of her Arts and Crafts predecessors when she formed Atelier Janiyé in the 1950s with fellow graduates of the School of the Museum of Fine

FIG. 50
In this necklace, Miyé Matsukata highlights the depth and texture of the green jade and red agate by contrasting them with smooth silver mounts and a textured cast silver surface.

Arts. The collaborative studio environment encouraged creativity and cooperation, as had the earlier Handicraft Shop and SAC Workshop. Matsukata's progression mimicked that of Hale in both materials and conceptual style. Her earlier work combined precious and nonprecious materials in a spare geometric abstract aesthetic (fig. 50). Her later work, as represented by a print of a design drawing of a gold necklace from 1975, took on greater complexity and fluidity, with more color and painterly effects (fig. 51). She introduced enamel as a way to play further with material properties and textures, much as the Boston Arts and Crafts jewelry makers had done.[8] While their creations had their own aesthetic, Boston's studio jewelers continued to draw upon the ideals and methods of practice of Boston's Arts and Crafts jewelry makers for many generations.

Arts and Crafts ideals can still be seen in jewelry making and other artistic communities in Boston and throughout the country today. Current artists and their patrons promote independent handcraftsmanship, in reaction to the dominance of technology and the isolation of the internet age. Regional and national efforts to support the artisanal movement encourage consumers to "Shop Small," "Buy Local," "Go Green," or "DIY" (do it yourself), further democratizing interest in craft. Artists and artisans have harnessed the power of the internet and social media to connect with buyers through websites and apps such as Artful Home, Amazon Handmade, or Instagram. Arts and crafts are seen as a way to reinstate person-to-person contact in an increasingly virtual world.

Once again, Boston and its environs have become a national center for handmade jewelry, largely due to the strong training programs at the Massachusetts College of Art and Design (formerly Massachusetts Normal Art School), the School of the Museum of Fine Arts (now run by Tufts University), and the Rhode Island School of Design. The supportive environment in Boston is also fostered by the ongoing leadership and mentoring of the still-vital Society of Arts and Crafts, which features artists' work on its website and gallery, holds a biennial jewelry exhibition, and connects artists and patrons at CraftBoston, an annual craft fair.[9]

Most recently, the practice of "craftivism" (craft + activism), which emerged in the early years of the twenty-first century, has resurrected the Arts and Crafts belief that crafts could be used to reform society. One definition of the movement is as "the practice of engaged creativity, especially regarding political or social causes. By using their creative energy to help make the world a better place, craftivists help bring about positive change via personalized activism. Craftivism allows practitioners to customize

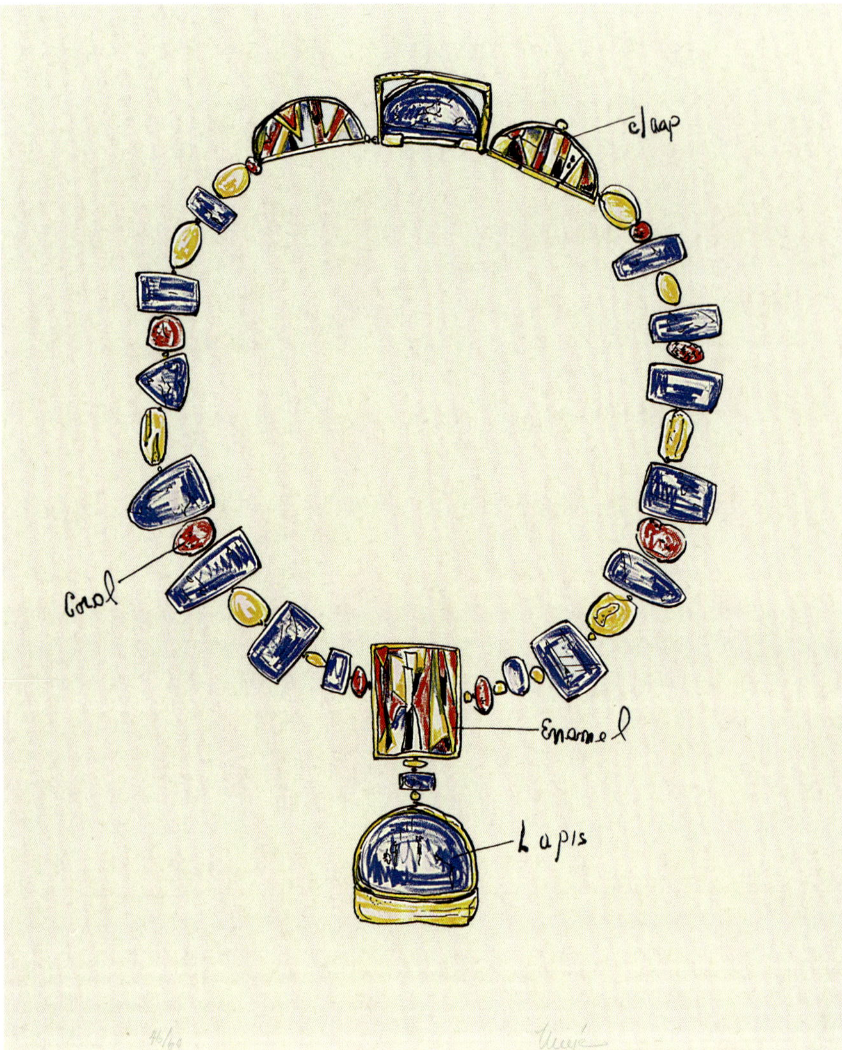

FIG. 51
A limited edition print of Maksukata's design drawing shows her later, more complex style that emphasized brighter colors and included enamel.

their particular skills to address particular causes."[10] The jewelry makers and metalsmiths Susan Kingsley and Christina Miller founded Ethical Metalsmiths in 2004 to raise awareness about the social and environmental harm caused by mining and manufacturing practices. They promote responsible material sourcing by working directly with jewelers and metalsmiths to provide information, develop alternative sources, and mount virtual exhibitions that challenge artists to reconsider the origins of the materials they use.[11] More than a century after the Arts and Crafts movement was founded to revive and preserve handcraftsmanship in an effort to improve the general welfare and happiness of society, the craftivism movement utilizes craft to encourage public discourse and engagement with today's critical social issues.

The Arts and Crafts jewelry made in Boston embodies the spirit of reform that pervaded the United States in the early twentieth century. Combining the ideals of design reform, social reform, labor reform, and craft revival, art jewelry offered unprecedented opportunities for women and other non-elite artists to support themselves through their artistic production. With the leadership of the Society of Arts and Crafts, Boston fostered a thriving art jewelry community through education, training, and patronage. Out of these efforts emerged a beautiful and distinctive Boston style of Arts and Crafts jewelry, as well as enduring ideas about the value of good design and handcraftsmanship in a modern world.

ER HALE.

APPENDIX I

THE FRANK GARDNER HALE ARCHIVE

Meghan Melvin

The Frank Gardner Hale Archive at the Museum of Fine Arts, Boston, contains a substantial compilation of original designs for jewelry, photographs, lecture notes, press clippings, correspondence, and other ephemera related to the artist's career as a jeweler. The material remained in the family until it was acquired by the MFA in 2014.

Among the most compelling materials in the archive are scrapbooks containing original watercolor and graphite designs and photographs of Hale's jewelry—in particular, two large scrapbooks that appear to have been compiled after Hale's death, likely by his wife, Julia Dwight Hale (fig. 52). Almost all of the drawings have pencil annotations indicating materials to be used. The specificity of these annotations indicates that the compiler had access to detailed information from Hale's records or from the correspondence on which the designs were originally drawn. The drawings are loosely arranged by color of the primary stone or by jewelry type, rather than chronology; the organization appears to be primarily aesthetic, forming a visual record of Hale's oeuvre in scale and materials. Regrettably, dates and client names are almost never discernible, as the sheets were cut to preserve only the jewelry designs (fig. 53).

Although they do not form a complete record, the design drawings and photographs in the archive represent a significant portion of Hale's body of work. It has already been possible to identify or make connections with many known works of jewelry by his studio, including quite a few shown in this book. Going forward, the archive should prove useful in connecting

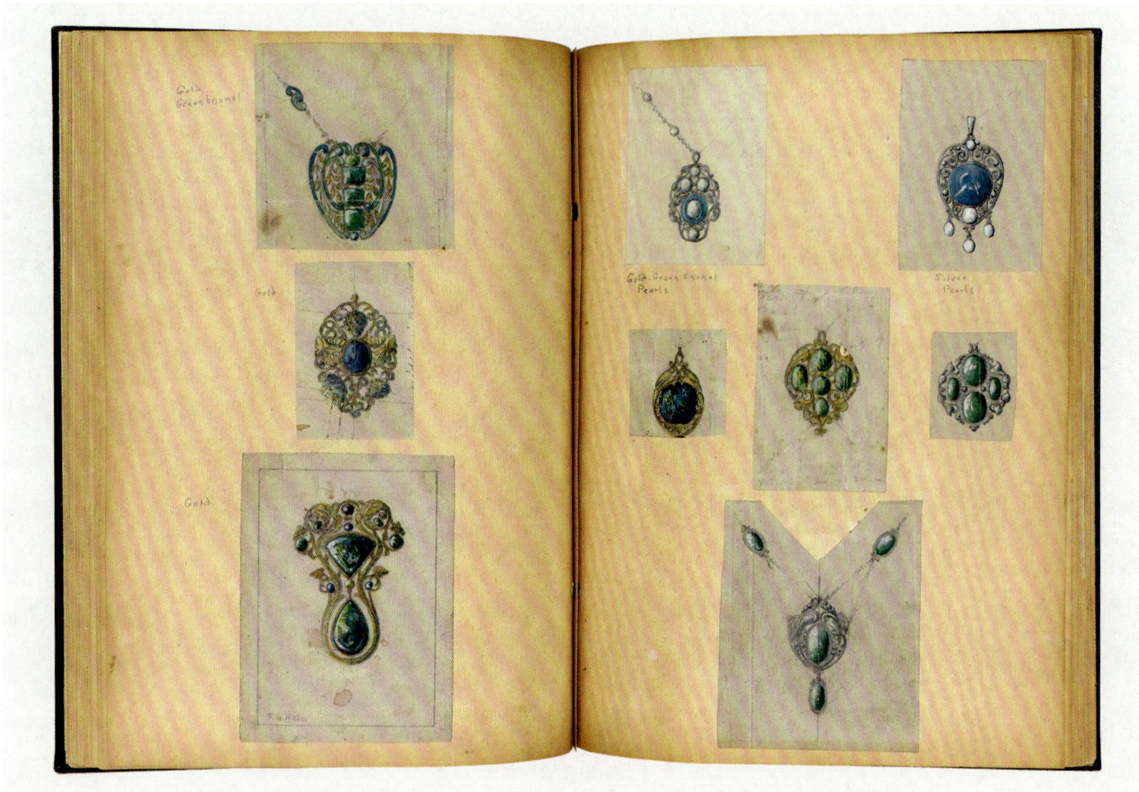

Hale with pieces of jewelry that have been hard to identify because they are unmarked, or because their marks have been erased by wear—especially the case with finger rings, which he designed in large numbers.

The archive includes a large number of pencil sketches for jewelry, likely used to capture initial concepts and record client specifications. These often give an indication of scale, materials, and decorations. Such drawings show that Hale worked closely with clients, both in person and by correspondence. Notes on these sheets of customers' individual preferences range from the weight of the piece to delivery dates (fig. 54).

More precise pencil sketches, probably used for reference in the shop, often have specifications for wire diameter, stone selection, and metalwork details. Some are to scale, while others are enlarged for production purposes. Most of these drawings are not dated; some, typically from 1913 or earlier, are stamped or inscribed with a date, as are a handful from later decades (fig. 55).

FIG. 52
Facing pages in a scrapbook show an array of designs for pendants with blue and green gemstones. The settings, in gold or silver, are determined by the shape, size, and number of stones.

FIG. 53
This working drawing for a gold and silver necklace set with peridot, emerald, amethyst, tourmaline, sapphire, and pearl (fig. 1) reveals the attention paid to the proportions and construction of the long sub-divided chain.

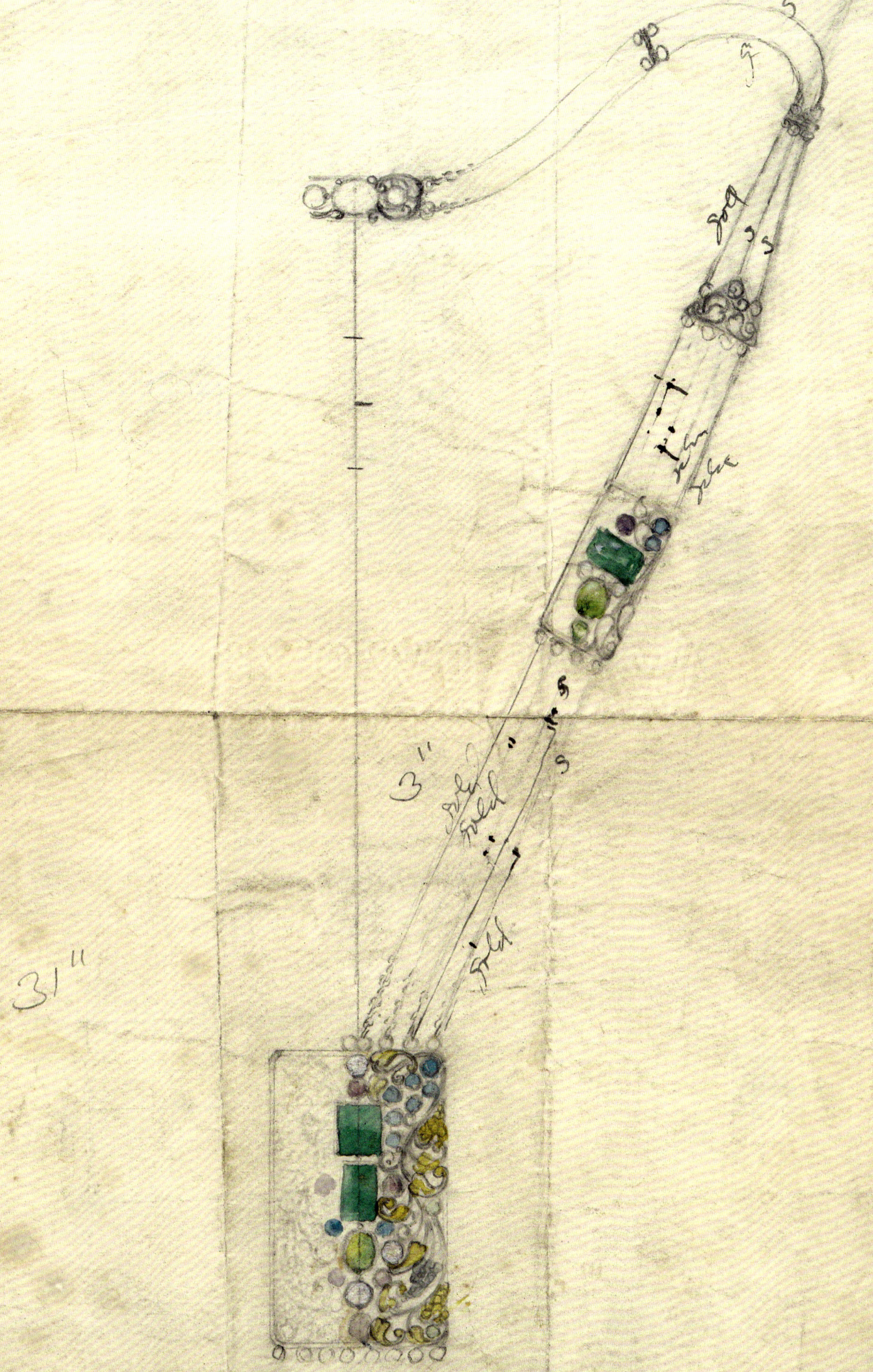
3"
31"

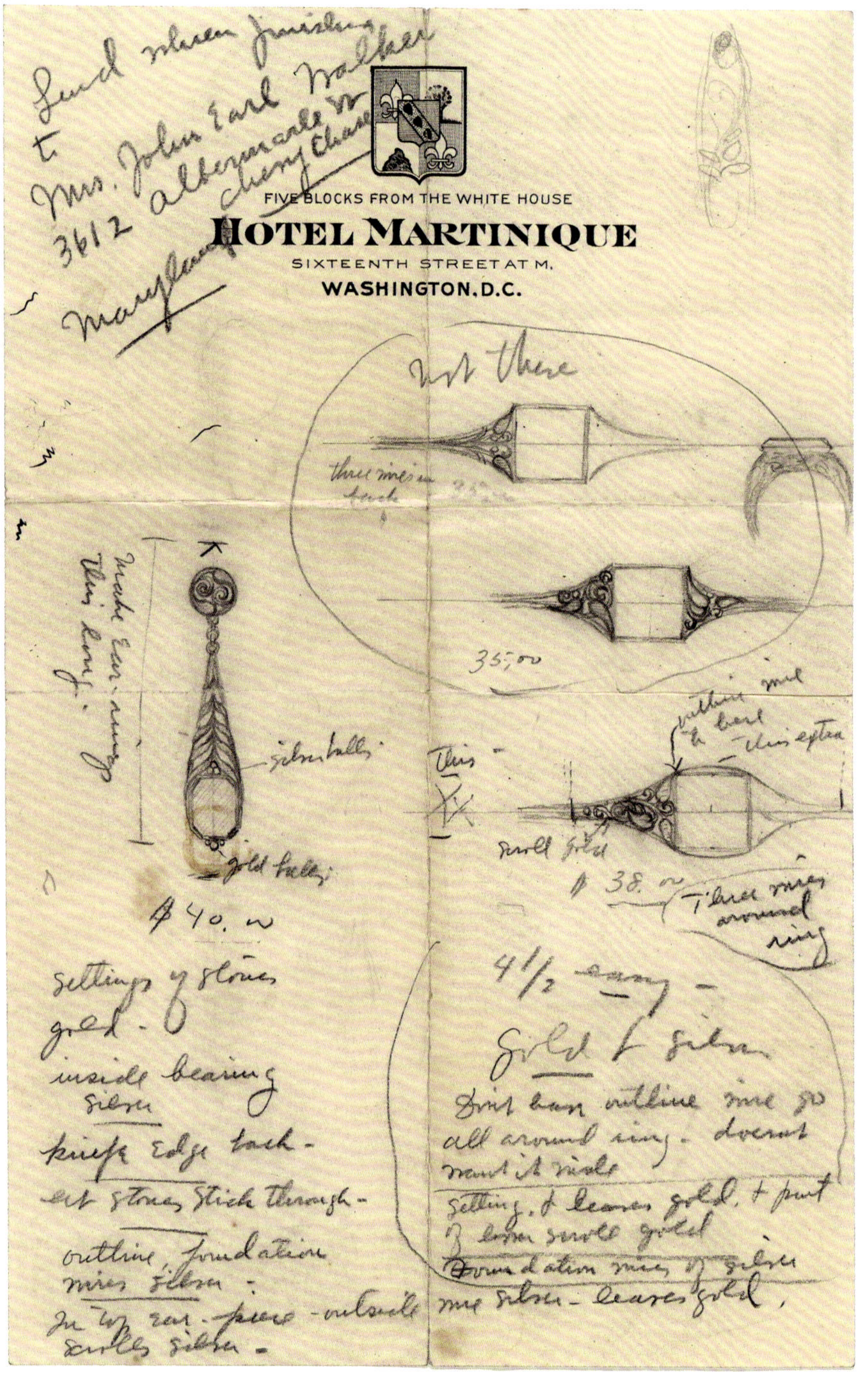

FIG. 54
Hale made regular visits to Washington, D.C., throughout his career. Here, detailed notes and sketches for earrings and rings appear on hotel stationery and record the stylistic preferences of a client from Maryland.

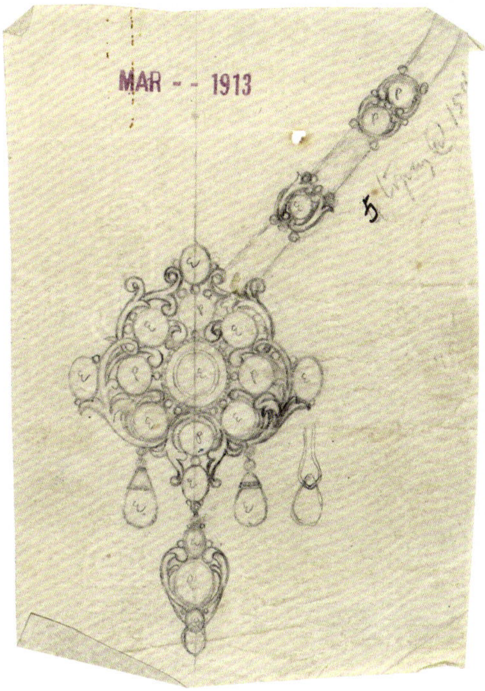

FIG. 55
A working design for a substantial pendant with an ornamental chain, likely a tracing of a presentation drawing, shows Hale's careful placement of stones: "e" may indicate emerald, and "p," pearl or peridot; topaz is noted in the upper right.

FIG. 56
Hale created many variations of this setting, which also relates to his earlier graphic designs. The version shown here is one of the more elaborate, with tiny diamonds or pearls connecting the outermost fronds.

Materials in the archive also reveal that Hale often created numerous variations on a theme, with minor changes in the orientation of central stones, the direction of scrolls on metalwork, or other aspects of the design. For a gold, yellow sapphire, and diamond pendant or brooch, Hale designed a variant with the outer scrollwork facing in the opposite direction (fig. 56; see pl. 2).

Many of Hale's final presentation watercolors appear to have been executed directly on client correspondence (fig. 57). Some of the correspondence, advertisements, and notes in the archive suggest that Hale's wife, Julia, worked closely with him, in particular after the business expanded to include retailing of antiques and textiles. The stamped request to return the drawing, as on this piece, was probably not always heeded. Despite his close communication with his clients, Hale acknowledged in a lecture that a gap in understanding could still remain: "The craftsman often meets a client who has so little knowledge of the possibilities and limitations of metals that he sometimes has to steer them away from demanding the impossible, and many cannot seem to understand a drawing." Many of the drawings pasted in the scrapbooks have adjacent penciled notes listing the pieces' materials. This information likely came from the letters that once contained the drawings, but the notations' spelling errors indicate that they were written by someone less familiar with gemstones than Hale (fig. 58).

Some of the designs show striking similarities to works by other artists, a reflection of Hale's attention to developments in contemporary craft in both the United States and abroad. The ship motif, seen here in a design for an enameled pendant, was very popular at the time (fig. 59). Hale had incor-

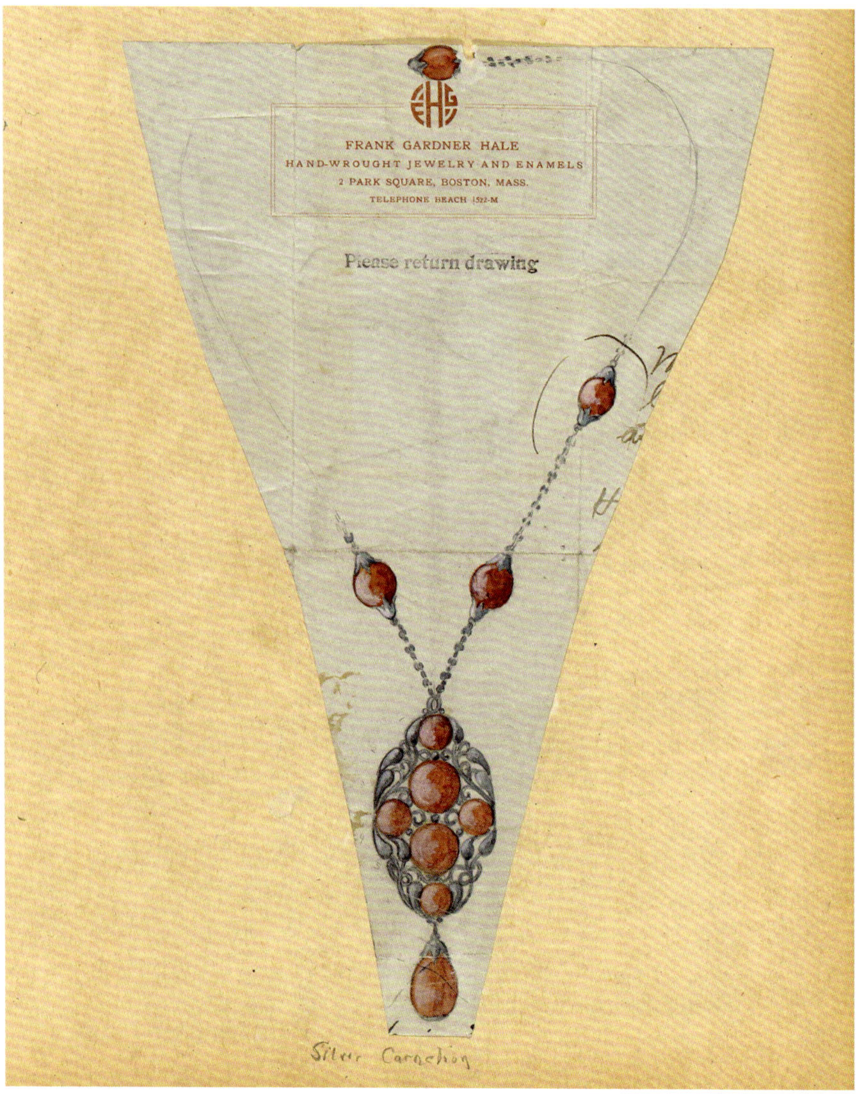

FIG. 57
A design for a silver and carnelian necklace extends to the top of the original sheet, with the decorative bead on the clasp drawing the eye to Hale's monogram. The position of the fragments of handwritten text suggests that Hale drew the design first, before adding his note to the client.

FIG. 58
Hale always took great care with the design process on paper, paying as much attention to detail for a small drop pendant as for a monumental necklace.

Silver Amithyst

Gold silver grapes-
Amithyst

Silver Amithyst

Silver Amithyst Pearls

porated ships in his earlier bookplate designs, so it would have been easy for him to transpose his design concepts into enamel (see pl. 31). Like many jewelers of the period, Hale also created a number of ecclesiastical works. His cross pendants resemble examples by his colleague Josephine Hartwell Shaw (fig. 60). Some brooch designs in gold embellished with diamonds and pearls recall the work of Edward Everett Oakes.

Taken together, the large numbers of drawings and photographs of jewelry suggest that Hale's studio created hundreds of pieces. A single traveling exhibition could include some one hundred fifty items.

Photographs of Hale's studios in the archive show that his training as an artist, graphic designer, and painter is reflected in his work environment as well as in his working methods. An image of his first studio-shop, thought to have been taken about 1909, reveals a well-supplied bench area alongside a comfortable office space suitable for welcoming clients. Examples of Hale's graphic design work can be seen on the walls above his bench, to his left, and a large safe clearly marked with his name is behind him (fig. 61).

Another important component of the archive is Hale's typed lecture notes, often with handwritten revisions. These indicate his knowledge of gemstones, art history, and jewelry making. They also provide evidence of Hale's individual aesthetic preferences, as when, in a lecture on "A Jeweller's Craft and His Environment," he writes: "Personally I am fonder of platinum used in combination with gold, for instance in a ring, using leaf, scrolls and perhaps flower forms—the stems may be gold and the leaves of platinum, and the petals of the flowers of gold with little embellishments of the more precious metal. In this way you have the lightness and the delicacy of platinum added to the warmth and color of gold, and this can be still further varied, by the use of different carats and colorings of gold."

A confident, detail-oriented individual and an able photographer, from the earliest days of his career Hale used photographic images to document and promote his work (fig. 62). Images that he sent out for publication are annotated with all the materials used, as well as with his full address. Hale

FIG. 59
The composition of the enamel decoration on this pendant fills the frame, creating a bold effect that is also seen in Hale's enamel plaques.

FIG. 60
Dense ornamentation on these pendant crosses is balanced by the soft color palette of the gemstones. The smaller scale suggests that they are personal jewels, not formal ecclesiastical ornaments.

Gold - pearls - sapphires

18 carat Gold. opal. sapphires & pearls

18 carat gold Tourmalines Sapphires - Amethysts

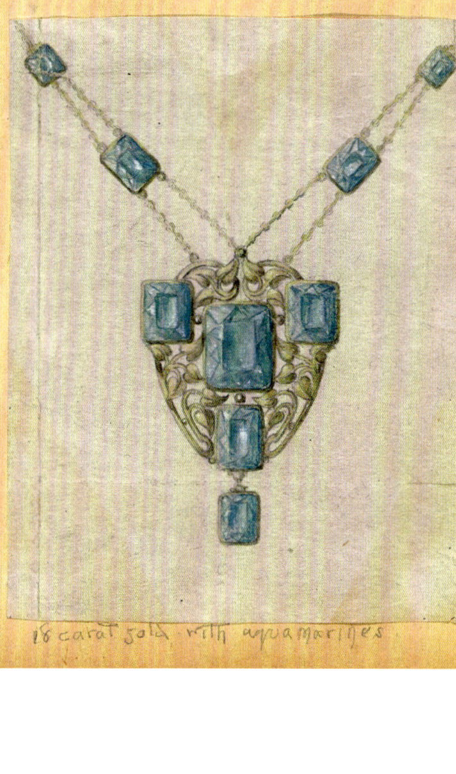

18 carat gold with aquamarines.

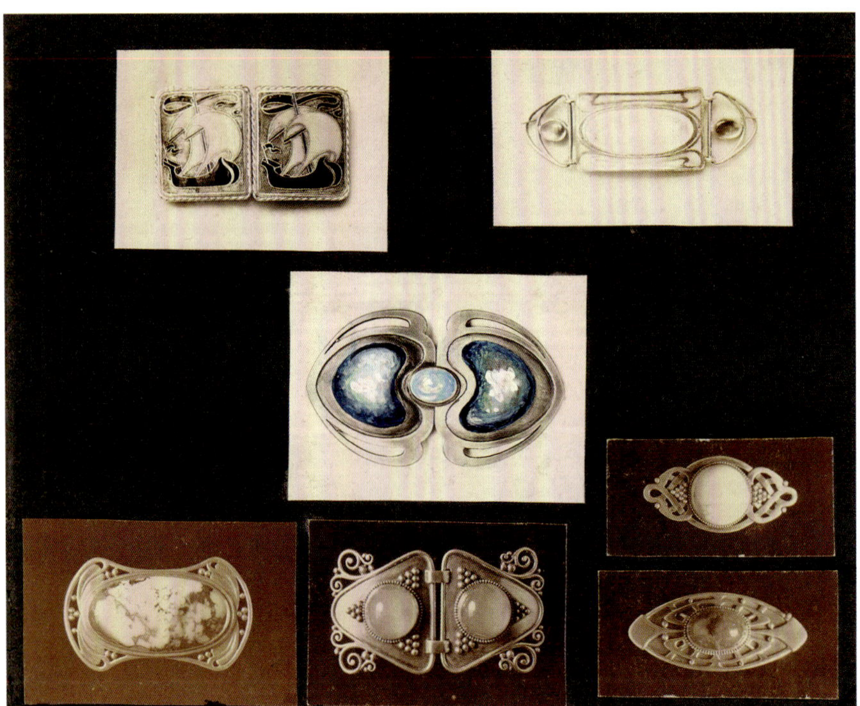

FIG. 61
Hale's workshop about 1909, two years after he began his career as a jeweler.

FIG. 62
An album of photographs of Hale's jewelry includes this page of buckle and brooch designs. For the buckle in the center, it appears that Hale cut out a design on paper, pinned it up, took a photograph of the drawing, and then tinted the photograph, going to great lengths to represent his original concept.

also hand-tinted a number of his photographs, even though they would not be reproduced in color. This likely was meant to convey a clearer sense of his works for those who could not see the actual objects. Annotations on photographs can help with dating some of Hale's designs, based on when he worked at various addresses.

The materials preserved in the Frank Gardner Hale Archive testify to his continued efforts to distinguish himself as both designer and maker, and reflect his desire for an independent identity as a craftsperson. They also provide valuable information about the artistic practices of the first generation of artist jewelers, who benefited from new approaches to education and training. The ability to draw well and to render designs in accurate detail was a vital skill for many artist jewelers. The Hale archive records in abundant detail the importance of design in the jewelry-making process, and the essential role of drawings for communicating creative concepts to clients or other artisans. It also demonstrates the consistency of Hale's design aesthetic; even as his technical skills developed, his style did not evolve dramatically. The archive documents this consistency and longevity of style, so typical of Boston Arts and Crafts jewelry, and allows a glimpse into the creative and professional life of a leading jeweler.

♡SHAW♡

APPENDIX 2

BOSTON JEWELRY MAKERS

Information is based on primary source materials including Society of Arts and Crafts archival papers and annual reports and government records found on ancestry.com. Dates derived from SAC annual reports reflect the calendar year covered by the report, not the date of publication. Locations are in the city of Boston unless otherwise noted.

LUCRETIA ELLIS MCMURTRIE BUSH (BOSTON, 1868–1951)

Joined Society of Arts and Crafts Boston in 1910, promoted to Master in 1915

STUDIO

214 Beacon St., Chestnut Hill (1910–27); 31 Trinity Place (1919–24)

Only a small handful of objects by Lucretia Bush are known to survive, but documentary evidence indicates that she was an active and prolific jewelry maker for nearly two decades. Born into a prominent Boston family, she spent at least three years of her childhood in Paris; as an adult, she became an active member of Boston's intellectual and social circles. She was an early member of the Daughters of the American Revolution as well as other prominent social clubs and charitable organizations. In 1900 she married the stockbroker Henry Sturgis Bush and moved to the nearby suburb of Chestnut Hill, where she raised four children and began making jewelry.

In 1910, at the age of 42, Bush joined the Society of Arts and Crafts. Within two years, she was regularly renting the showroom's exhibition space at 9 Park Street for solo exhibitions. An invitation from her April 1917 exhibition noted that her handwrought jewelry was of her own design. The brooch featured in this book (pl. 22) and a necklace that was published in *The House Beautiful* in 1915 are both made of gold; advertisements from 1920 and 1921 confirm that Bush also worked in silver and platinum, and that she refashioned "antique jewelry." A platinum ring featuring a large tourmaline, along with emeralds and diamonds, was included in Rhode Island School of Design's *American Handicraft* exhibition in January 1923.

ELIZABETH ETHEL COPELAND (NORTH CHELSEA, 1866–1957)

Joined Society of Arts and Crafts Boston in 1900, promoted to Master in 1909, Medalist 1916

STUDIO

294–296 Boylston St. (1904–36)

The metalsmith, enamellist, and jeweler Elizabeth "Lizzie" Copeland was born in North Chelsea (now Revere), Mass., in 1866. By the time she was fourteen, her family relocated to the nearby town of Bedford, where her father worked as a farmer and her mother kept house. At the age of thirty, while still living with her parents, Copeland began commuting to Boston to study design at the Cowles Art School with Amy Sacker and to train in enamels, probably with Laurin Hovey Martin. Later she took Denman Ross's course Principles of Design at Harvard. It was during her time as a student that she met a fellow artist, Sarah Choate Sears, who became her friend and patron; the two shared studio space for some time, and Sears sent Copeland for further study in Europe in 1908. While in London, Copeland continued her studies in enamel, quite likely with the celebrated English Arts and Crafts silversmith and enamellist Alexander Fisher.

During the early years of the twentieth century, Copeland quickly built a reputation locally and nationally. She participated in exhibitions at the Art Institute of Chicago's annual Arts and Crafts exhibit (nearly every year from 1903 to 1917), the St. Louis Universal Exhibition (1904), the Second Annual

Exhibition of the National Society of Craftsmen (1907), Society of Arts and Crafts Boston exhibitions between 1907 and 1927, Arts and Crafts Society of Detroit (1910), Museum of Fine Arts, Boston (1911, 1913), and the San Francisco Panama-Pacific International Exposition (1915), among others. In 1915 she was awarded the Mrs. Albert H. Loeb prize for "best original design" at the Art Institute of Chicago and the bronze medal at the Panama-Pacific Exposition for her work as an enamellist.

After fifteen years as a member of the Society of Arts and Crafts, Copeland was the first enamellist to be named Medalist, the group's highest honor, in 1916. Three years later, in 1919, Copeland became one of the first female contemporary artists to have work in the permanent collection of the MFA when it acquired a silver and enamel box she made in 1912 (see fig. 9). The Detroit Institute of Art and the Cincinnati Museum of Art acquired examples of her silver enamel metalwork in the same year. Copeland remained among Boston's most prominent enamellists until her retirement from the SAC in 1937.

JESSIE AMES DUNBAR
(CANTON, 1876–1956)

Joined Society of Arts and Crafts Boston in 1907, promoted to Master in 1912

STUDIO
26 Lime St. (Room 9, by 1911); North End Road, Monhegan Island, Maine (by 1919)

After receiving her diploma from the Department of Design at the School of the Museum of Fine Arts in 1907 and pursuing another year of postgraduate study, Jessie Ames Dunbar had her work published in *Art and Progress* (1913), *American Art News* (1915), and *The American Magazine of Art* (1916). In addition to exhibiting with Boston's Society of Arts and Crafts, her jewelry was also featured at other East Coast venues. In 1913 her jewelry was shown at the Handicraft Club in Baltimore, and two years later it was exhibited alongside works by Margaret Rogers and Josephine Hartwell Shaw at The Little Gallery at 15 East 40th Street in New York City. In 1923 her black opal, diamond, sapphire, and pearl necklace was included in the *American Handicraft* exhibition at the Rhode Island School of Design.

Dunbar maintained a bench in a shared studio on Lime Street in Boston's Beacon Hill, commuting between Boston and her hometown of Canton, Mass., before settling on a location on Myrtle Street—around the corner from her workshop—by 1923. During the summer months Dunbar left the sweltering heat of the city and spent time with family on Monhegan Island, off the coast of Maine. There, she set up a summer studio-shop where she sold her jewelry, as well as paintings, ceramics, and other work by local artists. Dunbar's surviving work is unsigned, but the jewelry handed down in her family demonstrates that she favored colorful gemstones in her gold and silver jewelry. In 1996 the Monhegan Museum organized the exhibition *Jewelry by Jessie Ames Dunbar*, which featured her jewelry alongside family photos and ephemera.

HAZEL BLAKE FRENCH
(BROCKTON, 1890–1972)

Joined Society of Arts and Crafts Boston in 1924, promoted to Master status in 1935

STUDIO

94 Jarves St., Sandwich, Mass. (by 1924)

After studying design with C. Howard Walker and jewelry with George Hunt at the School of the Museum of Fine Arts, Hazel Blake married Bertrand French and relocated to Cape Cod in 1914. They raised three children in the town of Sandwich. As part of her artistic practice, French scavenged for bits of colored glass among the ruins of the nearby Boston and Sandwich Glass Company, which had closed in 1888. She then would send the glass to lapidaries in New York for cutting and polishing and incorporate them in what she described as "interpretive jewelry set with old Sandwich Glass." Her silver, gold, and copper designs often include natural motifs of leaves, flowers, or seashells.

French's jewelry was featured in articles in the *Boston Daily Globe* in 1924 and 1925 and was exhibited locally. A member of the Society of Arts and Crafts for just eleven years, French participated in an exhibition at the Society showroom in 1925 and in the organization's tercentennial exhibition in 1927. Ten years later, a bracelet by her was included in the American Federation of the Arts Exposition International in Paris, and in the 1940s her work was showcased at the Art Alliance in Philadelphia. French taught metals and jewelry courses locally at the Sea Pines School and the Cape Cod Institute of Music, both in Brewster, Mass. In 2003, the Sandwich Glass Museum organized a retrospective exhibition, *Colors in Nature: The Glass Jewelry of Hazel Blake French.*

FRANK GARDNER HALE
(NORWICH, CONN., 1876–1945)

Joined Society of Arts and Crafts Boston as Master in 1907, Medalist 1915

STUDIO

400 Northampton St. (1907–12); 2 Park Square (1913–42)

After attending the Norwich Art School in Connecticut and the School of the Museum of Fine Arts, Frank Gardner Hale worked as a graphic designer, most notably creating sheet music covers for Boston's Oliver Ditson Company, before embarking on a career as an enamellist and jeweler. In 1906 Hale traveled to England, where he studied at Charles Robert Ashbee's Guild of Handicraft in Chipping Campden. Hale continued his training in London in the workshop of the jeweler Fred Partridge. In 1907 he returned to Boston, where he quickly became a leader at the Society of Arts and Crafts, being elevated to Master, serving on various committees and on the esteemed jury, and leading the Jewelers' Guild when it was established in 1918. Hale married Julia Raymond Dwight in 1909, and the couple resided in Boston, spending summers north of the city in Marblehead, Mass.

An active lecturer, Hale traveled throughout the United States giving talks about the Arts and Crafts movement and selling his work. Exhibitions of Hale's enamels and jewelry were held in Baltimore, Chicago, Boston, Detroit, Denver, Manhattan, Omaha, Pittsburgh, Providence, San Diego, and Washington, D.C. His jewelry and enamels received awards at expositions including the Panama-Pacific Exhibition (1915) and the Exhibition of Applied Arts in California (1917). From the start of his career, Hale employed assistants to fabricate his designs from notes and drawings, among them John Ballou, Edward Everett Oakes, and Gertrude Rosendahl.

LAURIN HOVEY MARTIN (LOWELL, 1875–1939)

Joined Society of Arts and Crafts Boston in 1899, promoted to Master in 1903

STUDIO

23 Irvington St. (Harcourt Building, 1900–1904); 400 Northampton St. (1904–10); 29 Exeter St. (Massachusetts Normal Art School, after 1911)

Laurin Hovey Martin is best known today for his enamel work, although during his lifetime he also had a reputation as a silversmith, metalworker, and jewelry maker; in 1907, a reviewer for the *Baltimore Sun* called Martin "perhaps the greatest handworker in metals in this country." After studying at Cowles Art School in Boston, Martin attended Birmingham School of Art in England, followed by intensive private instruction with the London enamellist Alexander Fisher. Returning to Boston around 1899, Martin established himself as an educator, teaching at Massachusetts Normal Art School, Rhode Island School of Design, and in summer programs at Columbia University, Byrdcliffe Summer School (Woodstock, N.Y.), and the Chautauqua Institute (Chautauqua Lake, N.Y.). He also wielded influence as a member of the Society of Arts and Crafts Jury, from 1900 to 1903, and through his published writings, including "The Art of Enameling on Metal" in the periodical *Keramic Studio* in 1905. In 1904 Martin married Harriet Nesmith Greenhalge. The couple settled in Martin's hometown of Lowell, where they raised two daughters, and Martin spent his career commuting between Lowell and Boston, at times operating workshops in both cities.

Martin trained a generation of enamellists, including Elizabeth Copeland, Frank J. Marshall, Mildred Watkins, Rebecca Cauman, and Gertrude Twichell. He also maintained an active artist practice until 1930. His work was exhibited at Rhode Island School of Design, Society of Arts and Crafts in Boston, Portland (Oregon) Society of Arts and Crafts, the International Exhibition of Decorative Metalwork and Cotton Textiles in Chicago, and in a solo exhibition at Charles Stuart Todd's Studio in Cincinnati, among others, and was published in leading periodicals including *The Studio* (1899), *Brush and Pencil* (1900), *International Studio* (1905, 1908), and *Handicraft* (1911).

Martin's enamels can be difficult to identify because he rarely signed his work; he experimented with a variety of materials and techniques; and his style was imitated by his numerous students. One trademark technique in his enameled bowls and plates is a heavy, dark ring of enamel at the rim, punctuated at regular intervals with descending triangles. While little of his jewelry has been identified, it was primarily made of silver and included gems such as moonstones.

EDWARD EVERETT OAKES (BOSTON, 1891–1960)

Joined Society of Arts and Crafts Boston in 1915, promoted to Master in 1916, Medalist 1923

STUDIO

44 Bromfield St. (Room 816, 1918–30); 145 Tremont St. (by 1931–37); 44 Bromfield St. (1939–44); 380 Albion St., Wakefield, Mass. (by 1944); and North Woodstock, N.H. (by 1922)

Raised in Boston's Dorchester neighborhood, Edward Everett Oakes abandoned his dream of an education at the Massachusetts Institute of Technology to become an apprentice to Frank Gardner Hale in 1909. Employed in Hale's workshop, alongside John Ballou, Oakes spent five years honing his craft while executing Hale's designs. After Oakes left Hale's studio, he continued his education under the guidance of Josephine Hartwell Shaw. Oakes may have worked winters with Shaw in her Duxbury, Mass., studio while maintaining ties to Hale during the summer months, when Shaw was occupied with running a teahouse. It was during this period that Oakes became a member of the Society of Arts and Crafts. In 1916 he married Irma Carpenter, and in 1919 the couple welcomed a son, Gilbert. Oakes taught on and off throughout his career, at schools in Boston and at his summer studio in New Hampshire.

Setting up his own workshop in 1918, Oakes hired his former student Elsie Parsons, who remained his longtime assistant. In addition to showing work in Boston, he also exhibited nationally at The Art Institute of Chicago (1918) and the Detroit Society of Arts and Crafts (1921). In an unpublished memoir, Oakes reported that he spent time as a Tiffany Fellow studying art and design under Louis Comfort Tiffany at Laurelton Hall, in Oyster Bay, N.Y. In 1928 the Metropolitan Museum of Art acquired a tassel necklace by him for their collection, and in October 1929 Oakes unveiled his masterwork, a jeweled box, in the Society of Arts and Crafts showroom (fig. 39).

Oakes's tenure as a member of the Society of Arts and Crafts was one of the longest. He continued to make and exhibit his jewelry in the Arts and Crafts style until his death in 1960. His son, Gilbert, carried on the family tradition; his work is marked with Oakes's oak-leaf stamp with an added acorn. Gilbert's daughter, Susan Oakes Peabody, and her husband, John R. Peabody, maintain the Oakes Studio today. Their work is stamped with the leaf and two acorns.

MARGARET ROGERS (BOSTON, 1868–1949)

Joined Society of Arts and Crafts Boston in 1904, promoted to Master in 1909, Medalist 1915

STUDIO

256 Boylston St. (1904); 108 Stratford St., West Roxbury (1905–8); 79 Chestnut St. (Silversmiths' Cooperative, 1908–15); 26 Lime St. (by 1916–38)

Margaret Rogers studied design with Vesper L. George and color with Albert H. Munsell at the Massachusetts Normal Art School starting in 1890. Munsell was an artist and educator who pioneered the way color was taught in Boston schools, and Munsell's system was later adopted more broadly as a way to communicate about color. From Munsell, Rogers likely learned about color matching, which is demonstrated in the arrangements of multihued gemstones in her jewelry designs. Rogers spent her life in Boston, residing in what are today the neighborhoods of Jamaica Plain, Dorchester, and West Roxbury, before becoming the owner of a home at 5 Sentry Hill Place, where she was living in 1924 when she applied for a passport to travel to Italy, France, and England.

Over her long career, Rogers exhibited with many of the other artists listed here. In 1907 she showed work alongside Shaw and Copeland in Society of Arts and Crafts exhibitions, and she also participated in the twentieth anniversary exhibition in 1927. Rogers's jewelry designs were featured in publications including *House Beautiful* (1906), *Good Housekeeping* (1911), and *American Magazine of Art* (1916). She also showed her work in Detroit,

Chicago, and Newark, and two examples of her jewelry were featured in the *American Handicraft* exhibition at the Rhode Island School of Design (1923).

JOSEPHINE HARTWELL SHAW
(WORCESTER, 1865–1941)

Joined Society of Arts and Crafts Boston in 1904, promoted to Master in 1909, Medalist 1914

STUDIO
4A Irvington St. (1906); 30 Ipswich St. (Fenway Studios, 1906–7); 9 Devotion St., Brookline, Mass. (1907–1913); "Three Acres," Duxbury, Mass. (1913–1939)

Josephine Hartwell had a successful career as an arts educator before turning her attention to jewelry. Raised in the central Massachusetts city of Worcester, Hartwell was educated at the Massachusetts Normal Art School and then at Pratt Institute in New York, where she studied with Arthur Wesley Dow. Later, she attended Denman Ross's design courses at Harvard. She taught drawing in Chicopee, Mass., Providence, and Philadelphia before returning to Boston in 1903, when she started making jewelry. In 1905 she married the sculptor Frederick Shaw, and together they set up a workshop at the newly established Fenway Studios building in Boston. While records indicate that Shaw did make some metalwork objects, she soon dedicated her artistic practice exclusively to jewelry. After her husband's death in 1912, Shaw relocated to Duxbury, a rural seaside town south of Boston. There she lived a dual existence, operating a teahouse for vacationers during the busy summer months and spending the winter in her workshop making jewelry. From 1914 until 1917 she employed Edward Everett Oakes as an apprentice.

Quickly rising to prominence once she began to make jewelry, Shaw participated in the Society of Arts and Crafts 1907 exhibition and held a solo exhibition in its retail shop in 1913. That same year she participated in the Society's exhibition at the Museum of Fine Arts, after which the Museum acquired a gold and pearl brooch and a gold, emerald, and pearl ring—the first examples by a female jeweler to enter the collection. Shaw exhibited her jewelry in Chicago from 1908 until 1918 and at the Cleveland Art Club in 1908, and it was written about in *The Keystone* (1910) and *House Beautiful* (1915). In 1914 she became the first jeweler to be awarded the designation of

Medalist by the Society of Arts and Crafts. By the 1920s, Shaw's production had slowed, and in 1939, in her mid-seventies, she retired from the Society of Arts and Crafts. Although Shaw was considered one of the finest jewelers of her generation, few examples of her work survive.

GERTRUDE S. TWICHELL (FITCHBURG, 1889–1943)

Joined Society of Arts and Crafts Boston in 1916, promoted to Master in 1926

STUDIO

15 Fayette St. (The Craftsmen's Guild, 1928–39), 44 Bromfield St. (Room 807, by 1941)

Gertrude Twichell was raised in the western Massachusetts town of Fitchburg. A 1910 census classified Twichell as an "artist," even before she enrolled in Massachusetts Normal Art School, where from 1916 until her graduation in 1920 she studied enamel and metalwork under the tutelage of Laurin Hovey Martin. After graduating with a degree in applied design, Twichell returned to Fitchburg until 1927, when she became a boarder at the Franklin Square House, a women's residence on East Newton Street in Boston's South End. By the 1940s she had relocated to a guesthouse in Brookline, Mass. From 1928 to 1939 Twichell maintained a studio at The Craftsmen's Guild, a studio-shop that provided artists with work and retail space. There she worked alongside weavers, printmakers, ceramicists, enamellers, and other artisans. By 1941 she had relocated to 44 Bromfield Street, in the heart of the city's jewelry district.

In 1927 Twichell contributed hollowware and enameled boxes to the Society of Arts and Crafts exhibition. She published an article on enameling techniques in *The Handcrafter* in 1929, illustrated with images of four of her silver and enamel boxes. She showed her work at the Detroit Society of Arts and Crafts and exhibited metalwork at the International Exposition of Art and Technology in Modern Life in Paris in 1937. Twichell is better known for her figurative and historically inspired cloisonné and plique-à-jour enameling than for her jewelry, but she interchangeably described herself as an artist, designer, and metalworker.

NOTES

THE RISE OF ART JEWELRY IN BOSTON

1 *Boston Daily Globe*, April 28, 1901, p. 33.

2 Irene Sargent, "Jewelry Styles Historically Considered," *The Keystone*, March 15, 1914, p. 86.

3 Elyse Zorn Karlin, "Early Twentieth-Century Art Jewelry," in *Contemporary Jewelry in Perspective*, ed. Damien Skinner (New York: Lark Books, 2013), 86–93.

4 Emily E. Graves, "Handwrought Jewelry in America," *The American Magazine of Art* 7, no. 3 (January 1916): 102.

5 A compendium of Morris's most famous lectures was published simultaneously in London and Boston in 1882. This quotation comes from "The Beauty of Life," a lecture before the Birmingham Society of Arts and School of Design (February 19, 1880), published in *Hopes and Fears for Art: Five Lectures Delivered in Birmingham, London, and Nottingham, 1878–1881* (Boston: Roberts Brothers, 1882), 110.

6 Many works by Thoreau and Emerson were reprinted in the 1890s and 1900s, as they continued to be influential. For more discussion of the relationship with the American Arts and Crafts movement, see Jonathan Clancy, "Transcendentalism and the Crisis of Self in American Art and Culture, 1830–1930" (PhD diss., The City University of New York, 2008).

7 Edward S. Cooke, Jr., "Talking or Working: The Conundrum of Moral Aesthetics in Boston's Arts and Crafts Movement," in *Inspiring Reform: Boston's Arts and Crafts Movement*, ed. Marilee B. Meyer (New York: Abrams, 1997), 17–31; William L. Vance, "Redefining 'Bostonian,'" in Trevor J. Fairbrother et al., *The Bostonians: Painters of an Elegant Age, 1870–1930* (Boston: Museum of Fine Arts, 1986), 9–30.

8 Such projects included the work at the Eliot School in Jamaica Plain to develop a manual training program for the Boston Public School system, and the Sloyd program run by Gustave Larsson at North Bennet Street Industrial School in the North End. For more information on the growth of manual training in Boston, see Nonie Gadsden, "Art, Craft and Reform: The Eliot School, Manual Arts Training,

and the Arts and Crafts Movement," lecture given at the Massachusetts Historical Society, October 27, 2016, available online at https://www.masshist.org/calendar/event?event=1931.

9 See Henry W. Belknap, "Jewelry and Enamels," *The Craftsman*, June 1903, pp. 178–80.

10 Martha Gandy Fales, *Jewelry in America* (London: Antique Collectors Club, 1995), 310–11.

11 Although SAC leaders believed and boasted that they mounted the first Arts and Crafts Exhibition in the United States, smaller exhibitions of its kind had been held previously.

12 Catalogue, First Exhibition of the Arts and Crafts, 1897; Society of Arts and Crafts Archives, Boston Public Library. For more information on the development of the exhibition, see Beverly K. Brandt, *The Craftsman and the Critic: Defining Usefulness and Beauty in Arts and Crafts–Era Boston* (Amherst: University of Massachusetts Press, 2009).

13 "Beautiful Things," *Boston Daily Globe*, March 29, 1897.

14 "The Arts and Crafts: The Trouble with the Present Exhibition," *Time & Hour*, April 10, 1897.

15 "Arts and Crafts Exhibit," *Boston Advertiser*, April 5, 1897.

16 Society of Arts and Crafts, Boston, founding documents; transcript available in SAC archive, BPL. For a detailed account of the founding of the Society of Arts and Crafts, Boston, see Brandt, *The Craftsman and the Critic*.

17 "Gem Making," *Boston Daily Globe*, July 28, 1907, p. SM7.

18 Julius Wodiska, *A Book of Precious Stones* (New York: G. P. Putnam's Sons, 1909) p. 270.

19 State of Massachusetts, Annual Report of the Department of Education, January 1902, p. 43.

20 "Handwrought Work Shown," *Baltimore Sun*, February 28, 1908, p. 5.

21 Frederick W. Coburn, "Metal Work at Boston," *The International Studio* (February 1908), pp. 145–48.

22 Marie Ann Frank, *Denman Ross and American Design Theory* (Lebanon, New Hampshire: University Press of New England, 2011), pp. 215–42.

23 Erica E. Hirshler, *A Studio of Her Own: Women Artists in Boston, 1870–1940* (Boston: Museum of Fine Arts, 2001); Jeannine Falino, "Women Metalsmiths," in *Women Designers in the USA, 1900–2000: Diversity and Difference*, ed. Patricia Kirkham (New Haven: Yale University Press, 2000), n. 23.

24 1905 SAC Annual Report, Report of the Committee on Workshops and Classes; despite the effort, the SAC design courses were short-lived due to lack of attendance.

25 "List of Books in the Library of the Society," SAC Annual Report 1918, pp. 20–21. Wilson's publication was positively reviewed by American jewelry maker Madeline Yale Wynne in *The House Beautiful* in May 1903, demonstrating its immediate impact on American craftsmen.

26 Arthur Astor Carey, "The Past Year and Its Lessons: An Address Delivered to The Society of Arts and Crafts, November 22, 1901," *Handicraft* 1, no. 1 (April 1902): 20.

27 Jeannine Falino, "Circles of Influence: Metalsmithing in New England," in Meyer, *Inspiring Reform*, 71–85.

28 In previous scholarship, the Handicraft Shop has been identified as part of the Society of Arts and Crafts. Careful reading of SAC annual reports shows that it was a separate but related endeavor.

29 1905 Annual Report, The Committee on Workshops & Classes, p. 16.

30 Names found in SAC Annual Reports and Boston City Directories.

31 "The Society stands in no different relation to those working in the shop than is the case with other members working elsewhere." 1905 SAC Annual Report, pp. 16–17.

32 For an in-depth discussion of the SAC Jury and its impact, see Brandt, *The Critic and the Craftsman,* chapter 3, "Adviser, Promoter, Tormentor, and Midwife: The Multiple Roles of Boston's Design Critics," 141–84.

33 1905 SAC Annual Report, Report of the Jury.

34 1906 SAC Annual Report, Report of the Jury.

35 Claire M. Coburn, "Specimens of Craftsman Jewelry," *Good Housekeeping* 43 (November 1906): 507–13.

36 See Irene Sargent, "The Worker in Enamel with Special Reference to Miss Elizabeth Copeland," *The Keystone*, February 1906, p. 193.

37 Belknap, "Jewelry and Enamels," 180.

38 "Designs and Makes Jewelry," *Boston Daily Globe*, December 13, 1908, p. SM12.

39 1907 SAC Annual Report.

40 The opening talk by H. Gustave Rogers was quoted at length in "Jewelry at the Arts and Crafts," *Boston Evening Transcript*, Dec. 9, 1908, p. 9.

41 *Boston Transcript*, as quoted in Frederick W. Coburn, "An Exhibition of Jewelry," *The International Studio*, September 1908, p. 85.

42 Coburn, "An Exhibition of Jewelry," 85–87.

43 1910 SAC Annual Report, Report of the Jury.

44 1913 SAC Annual Report, Report of the Jury.

45 1913 SAC Annual Report, Report of the Exhibition Committee.

46 "The Fine Arts: Jewelry and Enamels," *Boston Transcript*, March 6, 1913.

47 Graves, "Handwrought Jewelry in America," 103.

THE MAKING OF AN ARTIST JEWELER

1 It is possible that Hale entered the SAC as a Craftsman, but he became a Master within months. He is listed only as a Master in the Annual Reports.

2 Lecture notes, "Jewelry and the Craft Movement" (about 1922), p. 3, Frank Gardner Hale Archive, MFA.

3 An SMFA brochure of 1898 describes instruction in "proportion, the elements of architectural and decorative form, and the composition and application of ornament, together with its historical styles and development," and outlines a four-year course that concludes with "practice in the technical application of design during the last year."

4 H. Winthrop Pierce, *The History of the School of the Museum of Fine Arts, Boston, 1877–1927* (Boston: Museum of Fine Arts), 68.

5 The Boston Art Students Association changed its name to the Copley Society of Art in 1901 and is still in existence today.

6 *Boston Sunday Globe*, January 11, 1903, p. 1.

7 The archive at the Marblehead Arts Association (MAA) contains diaries of Frank Gardner Hale from his year abroad

in 1906–7 and his European vacations (1913 and 1933), as well as other ephemera. Hale was a founding member of the MAA.

8 To date the author has identified more than fifty sheet music covers designed by Hale.

9 Beverly Kay Brandt, *The Craftsman and the Critic: Defining Usefulness and Beauty in Arts and Crafts–Era Boston* (Amherst: University of Massachusetts Press, 2009), 114.

10 Charlotte Whitcomb, *Brush and Pencil* 7, no. 6 (March 1901): 352.

11 Henry Hunt Clark, "Frank Gardner Hale, Jeweller," *The American Magazine of Art* 14, no. 4 (April 1923): 189.

12 "Jewelry and the Craft Movement," p. 8; note in pencil, "when I went to England in 1907 it was not possible to study jewelry here."

13 Clark, "Frank Gardner Hale, Jeweller," 189.

14 Lecture notes, "A Jeweller's Craft and His Environment" (after 1926), p. 4: "Years are spent in study to add to a natural gift for one's calling, to understand the materials he is to use, its possibilities and limitations, to handle his tools, to acquire a real background of design, and to study at museums and by travel, the great things which have been made in other times, but not to copy them, but translate them into terms of your own." An undated newspaper article probably from the 1920s in the Marblehead Museum reports, "Designing bookplates and music covers for Oliver Ditson occupied him ten years, but the limitation of self--expression involved in it, finally made him decide to begin independently the making of artistic jewelry by hand work."

15 From the diary held by the Marblehead Arts Association, entry for May 18, 1906. All subsequent quotations from Hale's diary are from this source.

16 The founders of the Museum of Fine Arts, Boston, modeled it on the South Kensington Museum (renamed the Victoria and Albert Museum in 1899).

17 "Jewelry and the Craft Movement," 10–11.

18 At the start of his residence at Braithwaite, Hale's housemates appear to have been Will and George Hart, George Chettle, Alec Miller, and F. L. Griggs. MAA Diary, entry for May 26, 1906.

19 MAA Diary, entry for June 5, 1906.

20 Copy of letter from Armand Jessop, a commercial jeweler in San Diego, to Mr. Reginald Poland, 1926 or later; from a scrapbook in the Marblehead Arts Association archive.

21 Photographs of these early objects are in the Hale archive at the MFA.

22 See a review of the exhibition, Florence S. Berryman, "Hand-Wrought Jewelry," *The Sunday Star*, December 14, 1941; preserved in a scrapbook in the MAA archive.

23 Hale made an appointment for Sunday, October 14, 1906, to discuss lessons. He visited Nancy Agar and her future husband, John Bonnor. Both were jewelers and enamellists who had studied at the Central School of Arts and Crafts under the tutelage of Henry Wilson. At this time, Bonnor was head of the metalwork shop at the Artificer's Guild, recently under management of Montague Fordham Ltd.

24 Hortense Corey, article in the *San Diego Union*, February 27, 1932.

25 See *American Art News*, Dec. 28, 1907.

26 *American Art News* 6, no. 24 (March 1908): 2.

27 Association with Marjorie Whitney reported in the *Lawrence Journal World*, May 30, 1936, p. 8.

THE BOSTON LOOK AND ITS CREATORS

1 "Design reform was not the product of craftspeople working in isolation." Beverly K. Brandt, *The Craftsman and the Critic: Defining Usefulness and Beauty in Arts and Crafts–Era Boston* (Amherst: University of Massachusetts Press, 2009), xviii.

2 The visionary document titled "Principles of Handicraft" opened each annual report for the Society of Arts and Crafts and offered five guiding principles for members: motives, conditions, artistic cooperation, social cooperation, and results. It concluded with the assertion "It is only possible to answer for the final truth of principles, not for the direct success of plans," emphasizing the importance of the movement's ideas.

3 Denman Ross, *A Theory of Pure Design: Harmony, Balance, Rhythm* (Boston: Houghton Mifflin, 1907), 193.

4 Advertisements from the 1907 SAC exhibition catalogue indicate that many craftsmen also worked as teachers of metalwork, jewelry, and design. Alice J. Morse, who described herself as "Formerly Director of the Department of Design at Drexel Institute in Philadelphia," sought students in design theory and practice at her Joy Street address; Amy M. Sacker taught "Decorative Design" on Beacon Street; and Ella Fairbanks offered design education as well as classes in porcelain decorating and watercolor.

5 Kaitlin Schinnick describes these as her "most ambitious" and "successful" years; see "The Jewelry of Josephine Hartwell Shaw" (Master's thesis, Bard Graduate Center, 2008), 3.

6 Ralph Bergengren, "Some Jewels and a Landscape," *House Beautiful* (April 1915): 149; Edward Everett Oakes, untitled manuscript, 1951–52, Edward Everett Oakes Papers, Archives of American Art.

7 George Frederick Kunz, "Precious Stones, The Manipulation and Their Application in the Arts," *Handicraft* 3, no. 8 (November 1910): 302.

8 Undated manuscript, Frank Gardner Hale Archive, MFA.

9 See Edward Everett Oakes, "In Search of Precious Stone," undated manuscript, Edward Everett Oakes Papers, Archives of American Art.

10 See the section of the February 1907 exhibition catalogue, "Department of Jewelry, Society of Arts and Crafts," 21. SAC Archive, Boston Public Library.

11 1907 SAC catalogue, vii.

12 Lillian Purdy Goldsborough, "Jewels of a New Brilliance," *Vogue* (July 1, 1921): 86. At the end of the article (p. 92) the author unusually offers: "On request, Vogue will furnish the names of the shops where the jewelry described above may be purchased."

13 "170 Marlborough Street," Back Bay Houses, https://backbayhouses.org/170-marlborough/.

14 "List of Members," SAC Annual Report, 1916.

15 Frank Gardner Hale to Edward Everett Oakes, April 6, 1928, Archives of American Art.

16 Schinnick, "The Jewelry of Josephine Hartwell Shaw," 43.

17 Oakes, "In Search of Precious Stone."

18 Edith Alpers, "Edward Everett Oakes (1891–1960), a Master Craftsman from Boston, Massachusetts," *Jewellery Studies* 3 (1989): 73–79; 76.

19 Edward Everett Oakes, "My Belief in the Crafts," undated manuscript, Archives of American Art.

20 See Alpers, "Edward Everett Oakes."

21 See advertisement headlined "How to Get There," *The New Yorker*, April 16, 1927.

22 Emily E. Graves, "Handwrought Jewelry in America," *The American Magazine of Art* 7, no. 3 (1916): 102.

23 An exhibition, "Jewelry by Jessie Dunbar," was held at the Monhegan Museum, July 1–September 30, 1996. Our thanks to Jennifer Pye for sharing information from the exhibition, including research, press releases, and correspondence.

24 See *Colors in Nature: The Glass Jewelry of Hazel Blake French*, exhibition brochure (Sandwich Glass Museum, 2003).

25 "Glass from Mill Ruins Founded a Business," *Boston Daily Globe*, March 30, 1924, p. 6; "Uses Sandwich Glass as Gems in Jewelry: Mrs. French Invents Semi-Precious Stone from Bits of Ware," *Boston Daily Globe*, July 28, 1925, p. 24.

26 See Darcy L. Evon, *Handwrought: Arts & Crafts Metalwork & Jewelry, 1890–1940* (New York: Schiffer Publishing, 2013), and Sharon S. Darling, "Beautiful, Useful, and Enduring: Chicago Arts & Crafts Jewelry," in *Maker & Muse: Women and Early Twentieth Century Art Jewelry* (New York: The Monacelli Press, 2015), 183–223.

CONSUMING ARTS AND CRAFTS

1 Elizabeth B. Stone, "Observations of an Onlooker," *Handicraft* (June 1910): 82.

2 Marianne Carlano and Barbara Martin, exhibition brochure, "Boston à la mode," Museum of Fine Arts, Boston, April 26–July 28, 1991; Abba Goold Woolson, ed., *Dress-Reform: A Series of Lectures Delivered in Boston, on Dress as It Affects the Health of Women* (Boston: Roberts Brothers, 1874); "Ladies' Dress Reform Meeting at Freeman Place Chapel, Boston, Mass.," *Frank Leslie's Illustrated Newspapers*, June 20, 1874, cover.

3 Report of the Council, Annual Report of the Society of Arts and Crafts, 1905, p. 14.

4 Report of the Exhibitions Committee, Salesroom Report, Annual Report of the Society of Arts and Crafts, 1909; and letter from Josephine Hartwell Shaw, April 20, 1909, Society of Arts and Crafts archive, Boston Public Library.

5 "Notice," December 5, 1912, Society of Arts and Crafts archive, Boston Public Library.

6 Report of the Council, Annual Report of the Society of Arts and Crafts, 1913.

7 Letter and receipts in the Society of Arts and Crafts archive at the Boston Public Library offer evidence of a massive fund--raising campaign to open the New York shop; see also advertisement headlined "How to Get There," *The New Yorker*, April 16, 1927.

8 The same dress, jewelry, and accessories are clearly seen in more than one painting by Paxton.

9 Sarah Frances (Fanny) Frost adopted the stage name Julia Marlowe. She retained the name professionally even after her second marriage, to Edward Sothern, in 1911. The silver made by Arthur Stone bears the monogram "JMS."

10 "The Attleboros," *The Jeweler's Review* 32 (April 5, 1899): 436.

11 Grace Hazen, "Hand-Built Jewellery," *The International Studio* 57, no. 228 (February 1916): 120; Ralph Bergengren, "Some Jewels and a Landscape," *House Beautiful* 37 (April 1915): 149; Julia Marlowe Sothern, U.S. passport application, May 16, 1918, ancestry.com.

12 F. Allen Whiting, "Arts and Crafts at the Museum of Fine Arts, Boston," *Art and Progress* 2, no. 9 (July 1911): 263; "Arthur Stone," www.ChicagoSilver.com.

13 Hazen, "Hand-Built Jewellery," 117.

14 Brookline Historical Society, "Brookline History: Stonehurst, the Eben Jordan Mansion," *Brookline Patch*, September 1, 2017, https://patch.com/massachusetts/brookline/brookline-history-stonehurst--eben-jordan-mansion.

15 Whiting, "Arts and Crafts at the Museum of Fine Arts, Boston," 264.

16 Metal Worker's Guild Annual Report, Society of Arts and Crafts, 1908, p. 18; J. T. Coolidge Jr., Report of the Jury, Annual Report, 1910, p. 14.

17 "Designs and Makes Jewelry," *Boston Daily Globe*, December 13, 1908, p. 12.

18 Advertisement, "The New Costume Jewelry," *Vogue*, May 1, 1916, p. 8.

19 Ralph Bergengren, "Some Jewels and a Landscape," *House Beautiful* 37 (April 1915): 149. See also Lillian Purdy Goldsborough, "The Rejuvenation of the Heirloom," *Vogue*, October 15, 1916, pp. 126, 128.

20 Ostby & Barton advertisement headlined "Costume Jewelry: Fashion's Newest Note," *Harper's Bazaar*, April 1916, p. 21; Ostby & Barton advertisement headlined "Costume Jewelry: Fashion's Newest Note," *Vogue*, March 1916, p. 8.

21 "Designs and Makes Jewelry," *Boston Daily Globe*.

22 Carol Colbourne, "The New Jewelry Art," *Good Housekeeping Magazine* 53 (November 1911): 587–95.

23 Advertisement, "In Mrs Ehrich's Gallery Earrings and Costume Jewelry by Frank Gardiner [*sic*] Hale of Boston," *American Arts News*, April 1922. Referring to jewelry made of precious materials as costume jewelry was not uncommon in the early twentieth century.

24 Colbourne, "The New Jewelry Art," 589.

25 Frank Gardner Hale, "Good Taste in Craftsmanship. And the Craftsman's Place in a Changing World," undated manuscript, Hale Archive, MFA.

26 Unpublished manuscript, Edward Everett Oakes Papers, Archives of American Art.

27 Etiquette books offer insight into the evolving rules of dress. See, for example, John H. Young, *Our Deportment, of the Manners, Conduct, and Dress of the Most Refined Society* (Springfield, MA: W. C. King & Co., 1882), and Emily Post, *Etiquette: The Blue Book of Social Usage* (New York: Funk & Wagnalls, 1928).

28 Hale, "Good Taste in Craftsmanship," 7.

29 Colbourne, "The New Jewelry Art," 593.

30 Colbourne, "The New Jewelry Art," 591.

31 Frank Gardner Hale, "The Compensation of the Craftsman," unpublished manuscript, Hale Archive, MFA.

32 Lillian Purdy Goldsborough, "Jewels Flash the Extravagance of the Moment," *Vogue*, January 15, 1920, p. 96; "The Long Earring Swings into Favor," *Vogue*, September 15, 1921, pp. 76, 100.

33 Hale, "Compensation of the Craftsmen," 10.

34 Marjorie Hillis, "All Colors in Paris Fade into Black," *Vogue*, December 15, 1921, p. 36.

35 Frank Gardner Hale, "Short Talk before the American Federation of Arts Convention," Washington, D.C., May 14, 1930, Hale Archive, MFA.

36 Unpublished manuscript, Edward Everett Oakes Papers, Archives of American Art.

LEGACY AND INFLUENCE

1 Anne Webb Karnaghan, "Edward E. Oakes: Master Craftsman, Maker of Hand--Wrought Jewelry," *The American Magazine of Art* 17, no. 12 (December 1926): 629.

2 Kelly H. L'Ecuyer, *Jewelry by Artists: In the Studio, 1940–2000* (Boston: Museum of Fine Arts, 2010), 50–53, 88.

3 See MFA curatorial files for correspondence (October 3, 2017) between Meghan Melvin and Scott Erbes, Curator of Decorative Arts at the Speed Museum, who provided information and images of the Hale plaque in the Speed collection.

4 Horace E. Potter, a jewelry maker and enameller in Cleveland, was another key figure in the development of Cleveland as a center of enameling. Potter, too, spent several years training in Boston, at the Cowles Art School and with Amy Sacker. Potter may have initially learned how to enamel from L. H. Martin before he traveled to England to visit Ashbee's Guild of Handicraft. Jeannine Falino, in "Silver of the Americas, 1600–2000," ed. Jeannine Falino and Gerald W. R. Ward (Boston: Museum of Fine Arts, 2008), 362.

5 Bates was also recruited by Henry Turner Bailey, an artist also from North Scituate, Mass., who was the director of the Cleveland Art Institute. Mark Baldridge, "Kenneth Bates: Dean of American Enameling," *Metalsmith Magazine* (Spring 1988): 29.

6 Bates published three books on enameling during his lifetime; his first, *Enameling: Principles and Practice* (1951), is still considered a classic educational text. "Kenneth Bates, Enamelist, 1904–1994," 1963 Cleveland Arts Prize for Visual Arts, clevelandartsprize.org.

7 See L'Ecuyer, *Jewelry by Artists*, Introduction.

8 Damian Skinner, "Exhibition Review: Atelier Janiyé and the Legacy of Master Jeweler Miye Matsukata" at the Fuller Craft Museum, *Art Jewelry Forum*, January 9, 2012, artjewelryforum.org.

9 Marni Elyse Katz, "Jewelry's Big Moment: The Crafts Is Thriving in Boston, Thanks to Great Schools and a Community That's Wild for Handmade," *Boston Globe*, March 10, 2013.

10 Craftivism.com.

11 With thanks to Emily Zilber for bringing Ethical Metalsmiths to my attention. For more information, see EthicalMetalsmiths.org.

LIST OF ILLUSTRATIONS

Dates for objects are supplied when they could be established based on documentary or stylistic evidence. Dimensions given are the largest measurement of the object, whether height, length, width, or diameter. All illustrations in Appendix 1 are from the Frank Gardner Hale Archive at the Museum of Fine Arts, Boston, Museum purchase with funds donated by Jean S. and Frederic A. Sharf, an anonymous donor, and John Lowell Gardner Fund, 2014.

PLATES

1

Frank Gardner Hale

Pendant
Gold, tourmaline, and diamond
7.3 cm (2⅞ in.)

Museum of Fine Arts, Boston
Promised gift of Susan B. Kaplan

2

Frank Gardner Hale

Brooch
Gold, yellow sapphire, and diamond
5.5 cm (2⅛ in.)

Neil Lane Collection

3

Frank Gardner Hale

Pendant Brooch
Gold, enamel, sapphire, amethyst, topaz, pearl, and ruby
9.5 cm (3¾ in.)

Collection of Anne C. and David J. Bromer

4

Frank Gardner Hale

Brooch
Gold, sapphire, and diamond
3.8 cm (1½ in.)

The Susan Donald Collection

5

Frank Gardner Hale

Necklace
Silver, gold, pearl, tourmaline, and peridot
Overall: 47.8 cm (18½ in.); pendant: 4.4 cm (1⅗ in.)

Collection of Marilee Boyd Meyer

17

Josephine Hartwell Shaw

Necklace, about 1913
Gold, sapphire, and pearl
55.9 cm (22 in.)

Museum of Fine Arts, Boston
Gift of the maker in memory of her husband Frederick A. Shaw, 14.418

18

Margaret Rogers

Necklace
Gold, pearl, and chrysoprase
41.2 cm (16¼ in.)

The Susan Donald Collection

19

Margaret Rogers

Brooch
Gold, pearl, citrine, pink sapphire, and opal
3.8 cm (1½ in.)

Collection of Terry and Paul Somerson

20

Elizabeth Ethel Copeland

Brooch, about 1907
Gold, turquoise, and opal
3.8 cm (1½ in.)

Museum of Fine Arts, Boston
Gift of Jane Kaufmann in memory of Charles L. Kaufmann, 1997.160

21

Gertrude S. Twichell

Brooch, 1927–41
Silver, enamel, and citrine
11 cm (4⅜ in.)

Collection of Terry and Paul Somerson

22

Lucretia McMurtrie Bush

Brooch
Gold, turquoise, and pearl
2.5 cm (1 in.)

Collection of Aram Berberian and Rosalie Berberian

23

Jessie Ames Dunbar

Brooch
Silver, gold, red tourmaline (rubellite), amethyst, watermelon tourmaline
6.4 cm (2½ in.)

Family of the artist
Reproduced with permission

24

Jessie Ames Dunbar

Brooch
Silver, beryl, rose quartz, pink sapphire, citrine, peridot, orange sapphire, topaz, blue sapphire
3.8 cm (1½ in.)

Family of the artist
Reproduced with permission

25

Hazel Blake French

Necklace
Silver and glass
Overall: 42 cm (16½ in.); pendant: 4 cm (1¾ in.)

Collection of Marilee Boyd Meyer

26

Frank Gardner Hale

Necklace
Gold, enamel, emerald, and jade
Overall: 47 cm (18½ in.); pendant: 11.5 cm (4½ in.)

Collection of Barrie and Deedee Wigmore

27

Frank Gardner Hale

Necklace, 1920–25
Silver, gold, and lapis lazuli
Overall: 65.4 cm (25¾ in.); pendant: 7 cm (2¾ in.)

Collection of the Newark Museum, Purchase 2004, The Member's Fund, 2004.17
Photograph: Richard Goodbody, © Newark Museum

28

Josephine Hartwell Shaw

Ring, about 1913
Gold, emerald, and pearl
2.5 cm (1 in.)

Museum of Fine Arts, Boston
Gift of John Templeman Coolidge, Jr. and others, 13.1699

29

Margaret Rogers

Ring
Gold, sapphire, diamond, and pearl
4 cm (1⅝ in.)

Neil Lane Collection

30

Frank Gardner Hale

Pair of earrings
Silver, gold, and carnelian
Each: 6 cm (2⅜ in.)

The Susan Donald Collection

31

Frank Gardner Hale

Belt buckle
Silver and enamel
Overall: 8.3 cm (3¼ in.)

Collection of Boice Lydell

32

Frank Gardner Hale

Brooch
Gold, diamond, and green tourmaline
6.9 cm (2¾ in.)

Collection of Marilee Boyd Meyer

33

Frank Gardner Hale

Brooch
Gold, pearl, and carved carnelian
4.5 cm (1¾ in.)

Collection of Terry and Paul Somerson

34

Edward Everett Oakes

Brooch
Gold, yellow sapphire, and diamond
2 cm (¾ in.)

Museum of Fine Arts, Boston
Gift of Mary P. Caron, David A. Paine, Alexander T. Paine, and Elizabeth N. P. Bell in memory of Jane A. Paine, 2013.4160
Reproduced with permission

35

Edward Everett Oakes

Brooch
Gold, platinum, diamond, and sapphire
4.8 cm (1⅞ in.)

Collection of Terry and Paul Somerson
Reproduced with permission

36

Edward Everett Oakes

Brooch
Silver, malachite, and pearl
3 cm (1⅛ in.)

Collection of Terry and Paul Somerson
Reproduced with permission

37

Edward Everett Oakes

Brooch
Gold, diamond, sapphire
5.7 cm (2¼ in.)

Collection of Terry and Paul Somerson
Reproduced with permission

38

Frank Gardner Hale

Brooch
Silver and amethyst
6.5 cm (2⅜ in.)

Collection of Terry and Paul Somerson

39

Frank Gardner Hale

Brooch
Silver and amethyst
3.8 cm (1½ in.)

Collection of Terry and Paul Somerson

40

Margaret Rogers

Brooch
Silver, colorless sapphire, sapphire, red tourmaline, pearl, amethyst, opal, and yellow zircon
4.7 cm (1⅞ in.)

The Susan Donald Collection

41

Margaret Rogers

Necklace, about 1911
Silver, amethyst, aquamarine, pearl
42 cm (16½ in.)

The Susan Donald Collection

42

Josephine Hartwell Shaw

Necklace, 1910–18
Silver and pearl
Overall: 56.2 cm (22⅛ in.); pendant: 6.7 cm (2⅝ in.)

The Susan Donald Collection

43

Edward Everett Oakes

Necklace, about 1923
Gold and agate
Overall: 39 cm (15⅜ in.); pendant: 5 cm (2 in.)

The Susan Donald Collection
Reproduced with permission

FIGURE ILLUSTRATIONS

FIG. 1

Frank Gardner Hale (American, 1876–1945)

Necklace, about 1920
Gold, silver, sapphire, emerald, amethyst, tourmaline, peridot, and pearl
Overall: 106.7 cm (42 in.); pendant: 8.25 cm (3¼ in.)

The Metropolitan Museum of Art
Gift of Jacqueline Loewe Fowler, 2014

FIG. 2

Frank Gardner Hale

Brooch
Gold, zircon, diamond, sapphire, and peridot
6.6 cm (2⅝ in.)

Museum of Fine Arts, Boston
Gift of Joseph B. and Edith Alpers, 1998.569

FIG. 3

Designed by Will B. Hunt (American, dates unknown)

First Exhibition of the Arts and Crafts poster, 1897
Printed by Thomas P. Smith Printing Co.
Color print or letterpress on gray artist's board
42.5 cm (16¾ in.)

American Art Posters Collection, Boston Public Library

FIG. 4

Unknown photographer

The First Exhibition of the Society of Arts and Crafts, Copley Hall, Boston, 1897

Society of Arts and Crafts, Boston Records, Boston Public Library

FIG. 5

Marcus & Co. (American, active 1892–1941)

Necklace, about 1910
Gold, opal, demantoid garnet, and diamond

Overall: 58.4 cm (23 in.); pendant: 8.9 cm (3½ in.)

Museum of Fine Arts, Boston
Museum purchase with funds donated by the Rita J. and Stanley H. Kaplan Family Foundation, 2013.1521
Image courtesy of Skinner, Inc., www.skinnerinc.com

FIG. 6

Made by Arthur Stone (American, born in England, 1847–1938) and William Blair (American, active 1908–9)
Designed by R. Clipston Sturgis (American, 1860–1951)

Sarah Wyman Whitman memorial chalice, 1905
Gold-plated silver, alexandrite chrysoberyl, sapphire, tourmaline, cat's-eye chrysoberyl, citrine quartz, spinel, pyrope garnet, grossular garnet [hessonite], pink sapphire, and yellow sapphire
21 cm (8¼ in.)

Trinity Church, Boston

FIG. 7

Laurin Hovey Martin

Round box
Enamel on copper
14.6 cm (5¾ in.)

Collection of Helen and Matthew Robinson

FIG. 8

Katherine Pratt (American, about 1891–1978)

Box, 1918–27
Silver, lapis, and enamel
15.9 cm (6¼ in.)

Dedham Historical Society and Museum

FIG. 9

Elizabeth Ethel Copeland

Box, 1912
Silver, amethyst, and enamel
8 cm (3⅛ in.)

Museum of Fine Arts, Boston
Gift of Mrs. Horatio Appleton Lamb in memory of Mr. and Mrs. Winthrop Sargent, 19.5

FIG. 10

Josephine Hartwell Shaw

Brooch, about 1913
Gold and pearl
2.5 cm (1 in.)

Museum of Fine Arts, Boston
Gift of John Templeman Coolidge, Jr. and others, 13.1698

FIG. 11

Margaret Rogers

Necklace
Gold, glass, sapphire, amethyst, chrysoprase, and citrine
Pendant: 3.7 cm (1½ in.)

Collection of Terry and Paul Somerson

FIG. 12

Frank Gardner Hale

Necklace
Gold, citrine, and garnet
Overall: 28.3 cm (11⅛ in.); pendant: 7.3 cm (2⅞ in.)

Collection of Terry and Paul Somerson

FIG. 13

Frank Gardner Hale

Design for a necklace
Frank Gardner Hale Archive, Museum of Fine Arts, Boston

Museum purchase with funds donated by Jean S. and Frederic A. Sharf, an anonymous donor, and John Lowell Gardner Fund, 2014

FIG. 14

Frank Gardner Hale

Plaque with depiction of a peacock
Enamel on copper
14 cm (5½ in.)

Collection of Boice Lydell

FIG. 15

Frank Gardner Hale

Necklace, around 1916
Gold, aquamarine, enamel, and pearl
44.5 cm (17½ in.)

Collection of Boice Lydell

FIG. 16

Unknown photographer
Frank Gardner Hale, February 17, 1899

Frank Gardner Hale Archive, Museum of Fine Arts, Boston
Museum purchase with funds donated by Jean S. and Frederic A. Sharf, an anonymous donor, and John Lowell Gardner Fund, 2014

FIG. 17

Frank Gardner Hale (designer)
Oliver Ditson Company (publisher)

Sheet music cover, *Songs by Charles Wakefield Cadman* (about 1910), detail

Museum of Fine Arts, Boston
Ruth M. Campbell Memorial Fund, 2017.4607

FIG. 18

Interior of metal shop, Guild of Handicraft, Chipping Campden, about 1905–6
From the personal photograph album of H. Stuart Michie (Canadian, active in United States, 1871–1943)

Courtesy of Thomas Michie

FIG. 19

Charles Robert Ashbee
(English, 1863–1942)

Brooch, about 1900
Silver, gold, blister pearl, garnet, and brilliant-cut diamond
13.5 cm (5¼ in.)

Victoria and Albert Museum
Accepted by HM Government in Lieu of Inheritance Tax and allocated to the Victoria and Albert Museum, 2005, M.31-2005

FIG. 20

Frank Gardner Hale

Designs for peacock pendant brooch, about 1915

Frank Gardner Hale Archive, Museum of Fine Arts, Boston
Museum purchase with funds donated by Jean S. and Frederic A. Sharf, an anonymous donor, and John Lowell Gardner Fund, 2014

FIG. 21

Charles Robert Ashbee
(English, 1863–1942)

Porringer with lid
Silver, enamel, and pearl
23.8 cm (9⅜ in.)

Museum of Fine Arts, Boston
Theodora Wilbour Fund in memory of Charlotte Beebe Wilbour, 1990.461a-b

FIG. 22

Designed by Charles Robert Ashbee
Made by William Mark (Australian, 1868–1956) and Adolf Gebhardt

Brooch, 1901–2
Gold, silver, enamel, pearl, moonstone, and topaz
10.5 cm (4⅛ in.)

Museum of Fine Arts, Boston
Museum purchase with funds donated by Susan B. Kaplan, Marshall H. Gould Fund, John H. and Ernestine A. Payne Fund, Linda Fenton, Dorothy-Lee Jones Fund, Penny Vinik, and Adrienne Iselin Gilbert Memorial Fund, 2007.827

FIG. 23

Frank Gardner Hale

Box with plaque depicting a moth
Silver and enamel
18.5 cm (7¼ in.)

Collection of Terry and Paul Somerson

FIG. 24

Frank Gardner Hale

Box with plaque depicting a water lily
Copper and enamel
18.5 cm (7¼ in.)

Collection of Terry and Paul Somerson

FIG. 25

Frederick Partridge (English, 1877–1942)

Necklace
Silver, moonstone, and enamel
Overall: 39 cm (15⅜ in.); pendant: 11 cm (4⅜ in.)

Private collection

FIG. 26

Frank Gardner Hale

Pendant, about 1906–10
Silver and moonstone
6.7 cm (2⅝ in.)

Collection of Rosalie Berberian

FIG. 27

Frank Gardner Hale

Hand-tinted photograph of necklaces and pendants, published 1908

Frank Gardner Hale Archive, Museum of Fine Arts, Boston
Museum purchase with funds donated by Jean S. and Frederic A. Sharf, an anonymous donor, and John Lowell Gardner Fund, 2014

FIG. 28

Unknown photographer

Edward Everett Oakes, John Ballou, and Frank Gardner Hale in Hale's workshop and studio, 1909–14

Frank Gardner Hale Archive, Museum of Fine Arts, Boston
Museum purchase with funds donated by Jean S. and Frederic A. Sharf, an anonymous donor, and John Lowell Gardner Fund, 2014

FIG. 29

George J. Hunt with jewelry students at the School of the Museum of Fine Arts

Published in School of the Museum of Fine Arts, Boston, Annual Circular, 1928–29

Archives of the Museum of Fine Arts, Boston

FIG. 30

William McGregor Paxton (American, 1869–1941)

Portrait of the Artist's Mother (Rose Paxton), about 1902
Oil on canvas
68.6 (27 in.)

Museum of Fine Arts, Boston
Bequest of Marian E. Phipps, 1987.548

FIG. 31

Unknown photographer

Jessie Ames Dunbar, Monhegan Island, Maine, 1920s
Photograph, gelatin silver print

Family of the artist

FIG. 32

Kalo Shop (American, Chicago, 1900–1970)

Pair of cufflinks, about 1920
Silver and coral
Each: 2.5 cm (1 in.)

Museum of Fine Arts, Boston
Gift of Susan B. Kaplan in honor of Emily Banis, 2010.682.1-2

FIG. 33

Necklace by Frank Gardner Hale (see pl. 26), in box with FGH inscription

FIG. 34

Cover of Guest Guide, November 11, 1928

Frank Gardner Hale Archive, Museum of Fine Arts, Boston
Museum purchase with funds donated by Jean S. and Frederic A. Sharf, an anonymous donor, and John Lowell Gardner Fund, 2014

FIG. 35

William McGregor Paxton

The New Necklace, 1910
Oil on canvas
91.8 cm (36⅛ in.)

Museum of Fine Arts, Boston
Zoe Oliver Sherman Collection, 22.644

FIG. 36

William McGregor Paxton

The Crystal, 1900
Oil on canvas
182.9 cm (72 in.)

Private collection
Photograph © 2011 Christie's Images Limited

FIG. 37

Frances Benjamin Johnston (American, 1864–1952)

Julia Marlowe, about 1900
Photograph printed from glass plate negative, 20.3 x 25.4 cm (8 x 10 in.)

Frances Benjamin Johnston collection, LC-J698-6452
Library of Congress Prints and Photographs Division, Washington, DC

FIG. 38

Edward Everett Oakes

Bracelet, 1915–20
Gold, platinum, diamond, and ruby
17.8 cm (7 in.)

Collection of the Newark Museum
Gift of Elizabeth Reid Walker, 2000, 2000.60.1
Photograph: Richard Goodbody, © Newark Museum
Reproduced with permission

FIG. 39

Edward Everett Oakes

Jeweled casket, 1929
Silver, green gold, amethyst, pearl, onyx; stand: laurel wood
20.1 cm (7⅞ in.)

Museum of Fine Arts, Boston
Museum purchase with funds donated anonymously, 2000.628.1a-b
Reproduced with permission

FIG. 40

Edward Everett Oakes

Brooch, about 1920
Gold, diamond, and sapphire
3.7 cm (1½ in.)

Museum of Fine Arts, Boston
Gift of Mary P. Caron, David A. Paine, Alexander T. Paine, and Elizabeth N. P. Bell in memory of Jane A. Paine, 2013.5111
Reproduced with permission

FIG. 41

Frank Gardner Hale

Design drawing, after 1912

Frank Gardner Hale Archive, Museum of Fine Arts, Boston
Museum purchase with funds donated by Jean S. and Frederic A. Sharf, an anonymous donor, and John Lowell Gardner Fund, 2014

FIG. 42

Louis Comfort Tiffany (American, 1848–1933) for Tiffany & Co. (American, 1937–present)

Necklace, about 1910
Gold, black opal, demantoid garnet, and sapphire
Overall: 36.9 cm (14½ in.); pendant: 6.5 cm (2.5 in.)

Museum of Fine Arts, Boston
William Francis Warden Fund, 2017.1328

FIG. 43

Margret Craver (American, 1907–2010)

Necklace, about 1934
Silver, yellow sapphire, and tourmaline
Overall: 36 cm (14⅛ in.); pendant: 4 cm (1⅝ in.)

Museum of Fine Arts, Boston
Gift of Margret Craver Withers, 1993.833
Reproduced with permission

FIG. 44

Margret Craver

Time necklace, about 1963
Gold and *en résille sur verre* enamel
Neck ring: 14 cm (5½ in.); pendant: 4.5 cm (1¾ in.)

Museum of Fine Arts, Boston
The Daphne Farago Collection, 2006.614
Reproduced with permission

FIG. 45

Frank Gardner Hale

Framed plaque with depiction of fish
Enamel on copper
Framed: 25.2 cm (9⅞ in.)

Collection of Boice Lydell

FIG. 46

Mildred G. Watkins
(American, 1883–1968)

Brooch
Silver, green chalcedony, and champlevé enamel
6.5 cm (2½ in.)

Collection of Terry and Paul Somerson

FIG. 47

Mildred G. Watkins

Brooch
Silver, enamel, paint over unknown material
5.5 cm (2⅛ in.)

Collection of Terry and Paul Somerson

FIG. 48

Kenneth F. Bates (American, 1904–1994)

Textures bowl, 1957
Enamel on copper
38.73 cm (15¼ in.)

Museum of Fine Arts, Boston
Gift of Kenneth Bates, 1990.482
Reproduced with permission

FIG. 49

Kenneth F. Bates

Study for *Textures* bowl, 1957
Watercolor, ink
31.8 cm (12½ in.)

Museum of Fine Arts, Boston
Gift of Kenneth Bates, APP.1993.2
Reproduced with permission

FIG. 50

Miyé Matsukata
(American, born in Japan, 1922–1981)

Necklace, about 1970–75
Silver, jade, agate, and carnelian
15.2 cm (6 in.)

Museum of Fine Arts, Boston
Gift of Lucy Fields, 1993.8
Reproduced with permission

FIG. 51

Miyé Matsukata

25th Anniversary Print, 1975
Lithograph
56.8 cm (22⅜ in.)

Museum of Fine Arts, Boston
Gift of Emily and Laura Starr in memory of Helen G. Starr, 2002.679
Reproduced with permission

JEWELER'S MARKS IN APPENDIX 2

DETAILS

ACKNOWLEDGMENTS

The Society of Arts and Crafts, Boston, was founded in 1897 to encourage "mutually helpful relations" among craftsmen, designers, and patrons. It is in that collaborative spirit that we embarked on this study of Boston Arts and Crafts jewelry, combining the knowledge and passion of curators, colleagues, collectors, and benefactors.

We are indebted to the scholars who tackled this subject before us, particularly W. Scott Braznell, Edith Alpers, Jeannine Falino, Marilee B. Meyer, and all of the authors associated with *The Art That is Life*, published by the MFA in 1987, and *Inspiring Reform: Boston's Arts and Crafts Movement*, published by the Davis Museum and Cultural Center at Wellesley College in 1997. Curatorial colleagues, including Vicky Kruckeberg at the Dedham Historical Society, Beth Carver Wees at the Metropolitan Museum of Art, and Ulysses Dietz at the Newark Museum, generously shared their knowledge and collections with us, as did the independent curator and author Elyse Karlin. Thank you to Eve Griffin of the Boston Public Library, and Fabio Fernandez and Luiza de Camargo, former director and curator, respectively, of the Society of Arts and Crafts, Boston, for allowing access to records that were vital to our research. Following a tip from Marilee Meyer, Lauren McCormack of the Marblehead Museum and Patti Di Carlo Baker and Betsy Hoffman Hundahl of the Marblehead Arts Association helped us track down diaries that Frank Gardner Hale kept while a student and apprentice in Europe. These previously unpublished sources allowed us to paint a fuller picture of Hale's life and early career. Darin Murphy and Sony

Prosper at the SMFA at Tufts Library facilitated access to SMFA alumni student records. Vivian F. Zoë, director of the Slater Memorial Museum, and Catherine Hale Harwood were also instrumental in aiding our research on Hale's work.

While this project is focused on Hale, it also sheds light on lesser-known jewelers working in Boston in the years before World War II. We are very grateful to Jennifer Pye, from the Monhegan Museum in Maine, who shared correspondence and files on Jessie Ames Dunbar. Similarly, we appreciate the time spent learning the details of Edward Everett Oakes's work from Susan Oakes Peabody and her husband John Peabody, and browsing through drawings and scrapbooks at Oakes Studio in Franconia, New Hampshire.

Many colleagues at the MFA contributed their support and expertise, including Mathew Teitelbaum, Ann and Graham Gund Director; Elliot Davis, John Moors Cabot Chair, Art of the Americas; Erica Hirshler, Croll Senior Curator of American Paintings; Anne Havinga, Estrellita and Yousuf Karsh Senior Curator of Photographs; Pamela Parmal, Chair and David and Roberta Logie Curator of Textile and Fashion Arts; Yvonne Markowitz, Rita J. Kaplan and Susan B. Kaplan Curator Emerita of Jewelry; Michelle Derrick, Schorr Family Associate Research Scientist; Richard Newman; Annette Manick; Katrina Newbury, Saundra B. Lane Associate Conservator; Mei-An Tsu; Thomas Michie, Russell B. and Andrée Beauchamp Stearns Senior Curator of Decorative Arts and Sculpture; Lauren Whitley; Jill Kennedy-Kernohan; Edward Saywell; Benjamin Weiss, Director of Collections and Leonard A. Lauder Curator of Visual Culture; Maureen Melton, Susan Morse Hilles Director of Libraries and Archives and Museum Historian; Greg Heins; Michael Gould; Saravuth Neou; Maggie Loh; and Anna K. Barnet, Jennifer Snodgrass, and the entire publications staff.

This book would not have been possible without the work of our team of volunteers and interns. Joan Brancale, Hannah Braun, Theresa Baybutt, Ariana Bishop, and Lauren Spengler assisted in transcription, combed through magazines, and were invaluable in gathering research and tracking down details for this book. Two former MFA Sharf Fellows from Simmons College, Lucretia Baskin and Alexandra Copeland, provided critical assistance with inventorying and rehousing the Hale archive.

While the MFA's collection contains a significant representation of jewelry by Boston artists, the archive of Frank Gardner Hale and our research revealed that these makers were more prolific than we knew. Time spent with private collectors, who generously shared their jewelry and metalwork with us, was invaluable to our understanding of these artists and their work. Thank you to Rosalie Berberian, Dorothy Beattie, Anne Bromer, Vera Champlin, Don Davidoff and Sue Tarlow, Neil Lane, Boice Lydell, Marilee Meyer, Helen and Matthew Robinson, Terry and Paul Somerson, Olivia Tarleton, and Deedee and Barrie A. Wigmore. We were deeply saddened by the death of Paul Somerson during the course of this project and are grateful for the all-too-brief opportunity we had to learn from him.

This book would have remained a dream were it not for the extraordinary generosity of Susan B. Kaplan and Jean S. and Frederic A. Sharf. These visionary benefactors supported the acquisition of the Frank Gardner Hale Archive, which sparked the conversations that resulted in this book and the corresponding exhibition. We cannot thank them enough for their unwavering support of jewelry and design at the MFA. During our development of this project, Fred Sharf passed away. He was a fervent collector of jewelry, scholar of history, and great friend and mentor to each of us. We dedicate this book to him.

Nonie Gadsden
Katharine Lane Weems Senior Curator of American
Decorative Arts and Sculpture

Meghan Melvin
Jean S. and Frederic A. Sharf Curator of Design

Emily Stoehrer
Rita J. Kaplan and Susan B. Kaplan Curator of Jewelry

INDEX

Page numbers in *italics* refer to illustrations.

MFA Publications
Museum of Fine Arts, Boston
465 Huntington Avenue
Boston, Massachusetts 02115
www.mfa.org/publications

Published in conjunction with the exhibition *Boston Made: Arts and Crafts Jewelry and Metalwork*, organized by the Museum of Fine Arts, Boston, November 17, 2018–March 29, 2020

Exhibition presented with support from the Rita J. and Stanley H. Kaplan Family Foundation, Inc. / Susan B. Kaplan, and Jean S. and Frederic A. Sharf.

Generous support for this publication was provided by the Andrew W. Mellon Publications Fund.

ISBN 978-0-87846-857-7

Library of Congress Control Number: 2018947528

For a complete listing of MFA publications, please contact the publisher at the above address, or call 617 369 3438.

Front cover: Frank Gardner Hale, gold, green garnet, sapphire, and opal necklace (detail, pl. 6)

Illustrations in this book were photographed by the Imaging Studios, Museum of Fine Arts, Boston, except where otherwise noted.

Edited by Jennifer Snodgrass
Production editing by Hope Stockton
Proofread by Kathryn Blatt
Photography research and permissions by Anne Levine
Designed by Ryan Polich, Lucia | Marquand
Production by Terry McAweeney
Typeset in Mercury Text (Hoefler & Co.) and Ideal Sans (Hoefler & Co.) by Tina Henderson
Printed on GardaMatt 170 gsm
Printed and bound at Verona Libri, Verona, Italy

Distributed in the United States of America and Canada by
ARTBOOK | D.A.P.
75 Broad Street, Suite 630
New York, New York 10004
www.artbook.com

Distributed outside the United States of America and Canada by
Thames & Hudson, Ltd.
181A High Holborn
London WC1V 7QX
www.thamesandhudson.com

FIRST EDITION
Printed and bound in Italy
This book was printed on acid-free paper.